ON BEING A PARENT

A PARENT

The Crash Course
In Character
Development

ON BEING
A PARENT

The Crash Course
In Character
Development

BEPPIE HARRISON

Bookcraft
Salt Lake City, Utah

Library of Congress Catalog Card Number: 95-75328
ISBN 0-88494-970-2

First Printing, 1995

Printed in the United States of America

For Geoff,
who has always been there

Contents

1

A Place to Start

Growing Up

Children ask why a lot.

So do their parents. Only we seem to ask why about the big, profound issues: Why don't our children get with the program? Why do they dig in their heels stubbornly on the most peculiar issues? Why don't they ever pick up their junk that festoons the house without somebody shouting at them? Why can't they pay attention to things the first or the second or even the fourteenth time you tell them? Why are they so consistently self-absorbed? Why do they crab at each other—and us—and make such dumb decisions and resist our loving guidance so ungratefully? Why does being a parent have to be so *hard?*

Of course, it isn't all hard, and in our quieter, more rational moments, we know that. The trouble—at least at our house—is that even after long years of experience to teach me otherwise, I still cling to the wistful notion that the periods of peace and tranquility are what's normal;

and when one of those intervals is going on, I feel that we are simply functioning properly and take the peace for granted, and then am disappointed all over again when the old familiar volcano, with or without any warning rumbles, blasts loose and peace and tranquility are once more in mighty short supply.

The nice times, the Norman Rockwell moments, are very nice, and we all get them. We know what it's like to watch a baby happily discovering the world, even if the bit of it the baby is concentrating on at the moment is a fluff of dust carefully retrieved with infant determination from under the couch. We tiptoe into bedrooms to check that all's well, and drink in the sweetness of a toddler, flushed and sleeping crosswise in the first big bed. No doubt you know the lumpy tenderness of holding a child on your lap when he's almost too big to fit but still craves moments of the physical comfort of leaning against you. You may know the satisfaction of seeing two or more of your children harmoniously and contentedly working on some project together, whether the project is a game or some parent-imposed task, and you can watch the relationship you hope they will have for eternity being built before your eyes. And perhaps you know the feeling of relief when after what seems like ages of combat with your adolescent you are inspired to say exactly the right thing at exactly the right moment, and after all the prickly attempts at independence your child turns to you trustfully and at least one more time you have a chance to be Mommy or Daddy and kiss whatever's gone wrong at least temporarily better.

Well, I've got a Norman Rockwell watch, but that's as close as I come to having those moments be a permanent presence. For years I have found that state of affairs to be very depressing when I listen to lessons and exhortations that draw wonderful idealized visions of family life with parents and children purring along side by side, everybody behaving with perfect courtesy and kindness, and then it is suggested that this Nirvana is obtainable by simply observing very elementary principles of parental conduct. And who knows? Maybe that's true, but when I look at other families (particularly on Sundays, when they are ranged neatly in rows in sacrament meeting), I wonder if anybody else has the difficulties I have in getting those elementary principles of conduct put into practice. I wonder if anybody else gets tired and crabby the way I do, or if my children are the only ones to be obstinate and careless and thoroughly unpleasant to each other and me on occasion. Maybe so.

I suspect not.

In any case, whoever said it was going to be easy? Growing up—which is the process that we as parents are supervising and, we hope, helping with—is hard. If we don't learn that by watching our children, we surely remember the struggles from back when we were growing up ourselves. We have never been told by the Lord or any of his prophets that we were in for a golden glide in any aspect of our earthly existence. A major reason we came to earth in the first place was to face difficulties that would force us into making choices, and then our challenge was to make the right ones. We were never told that making those choices, even making the right ones, would mean we got rewarded on the spot with a round of applause and warm smiles from all around.

We believe firmly that, in the long run, making the right choices gets us a lot further. But in the short run? Well, generally speaking, few of the prophets or the other worthy men and women whose examples we find in the scriptures and elsewhere have had easy public lives (and of course most of the time we don't know much about their domestic arrangements). We do know the outside world was more often hostile than not: Joseph Smith was not the only one of our righteous predecessors to seal his testimony with his blood, and after his death his family struggled on without him and certainly had their share of ups and downs.

Living on this earth is often hard. It was meant to be. In a manner of speaking, life here is simply another stage in our spiritual growing up. It has often seemed to me that what we are really learning to do here is to take responsibility for ourselves. We know very little about our life before we came to this earth, but what we do know suggests that, because we lived in the presence of our Heavenly Father, we were to a certain degree insulated from evil. It was Satan's plan to impose on us his own form of insulation, mainly by not permitting us to make any choices at all. And, of course, he expected to get total credit for the resulting "successes." Fortunately, in terms of our eternal progression, Satan's plan wasn't put into effect. Instead, we indeed make choices freely and voluntarily. However, we also have to take the responsibility for the consequences that come with those choices.

Simply making a choice isn't that hard. What makes it hard is recognizing that your choice necessarily has consequences you have to live with. When the consequences aren't what you wanted, you can't just say, "Oops," and go back and choose again. Thanks to Christ's sacrifice, it is indeed possible to make other, superseding choices after you've chosen badly—a process we call repentance—but a lot more is involved than "Oops."

It seems to me that at the most fundamental level this is exactly what we're trying to teach our children. All the other things we're trying to teach them grow out of that. Even more fundamentally, we ourselves are still trying to learn what we're trying to teach, and it seems to me that, if I'm a typical example, parents certainly have days when they're only a very short step ahead of their children in the lesson plan.

That being the case (and I can assure you that in my case at least it is), it seems most odd that the Lord, knowing this (and I assure you that he does), would make me responsible for four vulnerable spirit children. Knowing that I'm not always so swift at making the right choices on my own behalf, how come he thought I would be capable of guiding and teaching them?

Well, the only conclusion I can come to is that it was certainly one very effective method of forcing me to sit up and pay attention. If I had been on my own, waltzing through life with nobody to think about but me, it might have taken me forever to get down to business when it came to character development. Instead, all of a sudden there I was holding a baby with a wobbly neck and trustful eyes who expected that I would be mature enough to take care of her. I had to grow up, and grow up fast. She needed a mother who was patient and unselfish and tolerant and all the other things mothers need to be. If I hadn't achieved those virtues yet, I had to get going. Whether I was good enough to be a mother yet or not, I was one.

Theoretically, the whole system has a splendid logic. It takes a father and a mother to produce a child. There are therefore supposed to be two stalwart mature adults who will shield and protect the vulnerable dependent children and shepherd them into independence, who will understand and provide what they need.

Well, so far so good. There we were, me and my husband, and we wanted our daughter to have the best parenting possible. It was that maturity business that was the problem. I had the sneaking suspicion that we had kind of lurched into the whole business. We were kids ourselves, overwhelmed and unprepared for how very much we were going to love this particular baby and how heavily the responsibility for her was going to weigh on our shoulders.

In those first frantic weeks when she hadn't gotten day and night straightened out, I was exhausted but determined to get everything right. I did have an uneasy feeling that the experienced mothers who told me this was the easy part were probably right; after all, at that stage all I had to worry about was keeping her warm and dry and fed.

The thought did cross my mind that the Lord could certainly have found a lot of women to give this child to who would have known a lot more than I did about being a mother. On the other hand, I was certainly unprepared to hand her over to anybody else, however qualified that person might have been. My baby looked for me when she heard my voice and she did funny lopsided baby smiles and she fit in my arms and I loved her more than I had ever dreamed it was possible to love. If I wasn't good enough to be the mother she deserved, I would just have to get to be good enough.

I guess the first time most of us grasp the full reality of what our parents felt for us is when we stare down at our first child and feel as if our insides are being squeezed with the intensity of our love and protectiveness for this fledgling spirit the Lord has entrusted to us to teach and guide and lead back into his presence. The enormity of the responsibility we've taken on—often light-heartedly, without giving it a lot of thought—is absolutely overwhelming. Without that equally overwhelming love to anchor us in position, I wonder if we might not be overcome by a temptation to simply run in the other direction as fast as possible, back to freedom and glib irresponsibility.

Thank goodness for that love. How does it happen so swiftly and so irreversibly?

If we believe the Lord usually works in natural ways, maybe the biologists with their theories can at least explain some of it. According to those theories, we are preprogrammed (at least in part) for exactly that attachment. As human beings, we give birth to large-brained infants, because in practical terms the neurological system has to be close to adult at birth. You can't learn unless you have a good brain to start with; hence human babies have as large a brain as can pass through the pelvis of an adult woman.

If an infant is born with a large brain, it has to have time to learn to use it. Therefore, the biologists tell us, human beings have a long childhood—a longer period of dependency than any other mammal. To guarantee that our infants will be nurtured during that period of dependency, human beings have a whole range of bonding mechanisms to "glue" mother and child together.

We know what the attachment to our babies feels like. Scientifically speaking, some of the mechanisms that go into effect to create that attachment are endocrinological and specific to the female: for example, when her baby cries, a mother produces oxytocin, which stimulates nipple erection and sets up the mutual satisfaction of nursing. Some bonding mechanisms are visual, triggered in both males and females by a baby's physical characteristics. Newborns arrive with physical configurations that attract us, the adults who will care for them. Babies have large heads in proportion to their body size; eyes that are large compared to their face size and that are positioned below the horizontal midline of their faces; and full soft round cheeks. They *look* helpless, and their helplessness appeals to us. (For very similar reasons, puppies are cuter than dogs, and kittens than cats.) When a baby appears on a movie screen and the audience goes, "Awhhhh," the awhhhh is only partially a result of social conditioning. Most of it is exactly the reaction that babies are designed to produce. It's a marvelous system to guarantee that the young of our species are protected during their immaturity and sustained and instructed during the years as they gradually grow into competence; it's a wonderfully practical demonstration of the common sense inherent in the Lord's plan for mortal life.

By and large, the plan works out as it's meant to. At the beginning, caring for an infant is relatively straightforward, as long as you can cope with continuous sleep deprivation. However, it can be guaranteed that adorable infants grow older and usually somewhat less adorable. They develop wills of their own, which in the abstract is a fine idea but is less appealing when it turns out that what your once-adorable toddler has in mind is sweeping all the cans off the shelf at the supermarket, and when you attempt to prevent him from carrying out this project his method of influencing you to change your mind is to throw a major temper tantrum in the middle of the aisle. If you're like most of us, you're taken aback, embarrassed, and feel like throwing a temper tantrum of your own to show this obstinate child who's boss. Only you're the adult, and you have to behave like one.

It's usually round about the time of the first super-market tantrum that we come to the conclusion that this child-raising business might be more complicated than we had thought at first. You would not be the first to find yourself thinking at this point that this is not a lot of fun.

It's also around about that time that most of us discover that we're not handling these new developments with the calm, adult wisdom we hope we are capable of on other occasions. We find—or at least *I* did—that a balky little round-cheeked toddler or a gangly careless schoolkid or a sulky teenager can reduce us to sputtering rage. Instead of handling the whole affair with mellow understanding, I found myself angry enough to have a frightening glimpse of how child abuse could start.

Ideally, parents are calm, compassionate, reasonable, and patient. In real life—at least *my* real life—there are days when I've lost my patience or my temper (or both), exasperated by what feels like deliberate obtuseness on the part of the children and frustrated by my apparent inability to communicate sensibly with anybody. Those are the days when I feel as if what I'm trying to teach the children is something I haven't learned properly myself. Those are the days when I've come to wonder whether the Lord's plan for parenting children is focused more on my children's immaturity or my own.

It was a parent-teacher conference that first made me think of that possibility. I was discussing current progress with a seventh-grade teacher I had known for years and who had taught all four of my children. Over the same period he also was engaged in raising his own five children, some of whom had been more of a challenge than others. We were mutually lamenting the pigheaded-ness of early adolescence, and our own slowness in figuring out how to cope with it, even after we'd been through the whole process repeatedly. (At least it's nice to know you have company.) We were companionably being amused at our mutual frustration, and then I suddenly heard myself saying, "You know, I really think the Lord means us to learn more out of all this than we will ever teach them."

Good Catholic that he is, he got what I was saying immediately. He raised one eyebrow and said he thought he was coming to exactly the same conclusion.

So what are we supposed to be learning, and why do we have to learn it this way?

Well, for one thing, parenting forces us to pay attention. For most of us, parenting is the most intensely engaging process we will get involved in during our lifetime here on this earth. Parenting grabs you right from the beginning, and it doesn't end. Back when I was coping with infants, I remember encountering a book which talked about the pitfalls of parenting adult children, and I thought in my new-parent wisdom, "Come now, they write the most preposterous books these days. Adult children? No such thing. They grow up and that's it. Look at me—I grew up." Well, my oldest daughter is an adult now by any definition, and am I still parenting her? You bet, and I have the phone bills to prove it. I now realize I'm going to be parenting from here on into eternity, and so is my mother.

Apart from your marriage, there is no other relationship that you are likely to care so passionately about as the one with your children. Oh, of course there are always exceptions: the newspapers are full of grim stories about parents who simply walk away and abandon their children one way or another, but the whole reason why those stories are in the newspapers is that such behavior is uncommon and unexpected. Most of us attach firmly to our offspring right at the beginning and stay attached from then on. (After all, the newspapers are equally full of heart-wrenching stories about custody battles of one kind or another between warring adults attached to the same children.) There are times when child raising would seem to be a lot easier on us if we could just temporarily disengage, stand aside, and let the children do whatever it is they have their hearts so set on doing. Unfortunately, particularly when whatever it is they are set on runs directly against principles we have tried our best to inculcate, the best we can usually manage is a feeble effort at pretending detachment, with the anguish leaking out almost visibly as we reluctantly admit that among our principles is a recognition of free agency.

None of us is fully ready for that intensity of attachment. Most of us don't give a thought to it before it happens. The Lord has arranged things so that usually we are fairly young and blithely unaware of life's complications when we launch into parenting. We're still growing up ourselves when we begin on it. After all, we all start out—ourselves and our children alike—as helpless human infants, totally dependent on others to supply our most basic needs and totally self-absorbed with those needs. Only gradually do we grow into our own strength and capability and start to look outward. Unfortunately, the business of looking outward is still very much in process when, about twenty years or so after infancy, we get catapulted into parenthood ourselves.

Parenthood doesn't change *everything*—the sky is still blue and the grass is still green—but it changes practically everything else. With the acquisition of a child (whether it be by the normal biological process or by a variation such as adoption), we find ourselves overnight in the middle of an emotional firestorm: we experience love, resentment, tenderness, fatigue, confusion, uncertainty, determination, and a hundred other emotions in no particular order or sequence, all mixed up and all together.

The muddle can feel overwhelming in the beginning. For one thing, everything else is usually in somewhat of an uproar anyway. Few of us are able to organize our lives so perfectly that the arrival of the first child comes when we are completely ready and prepared with the rest of our obligations neatly arranged so as not to be intrusive. Far more often there are loose ends all over the place. Maybe you live close to family; maybe you don't. Maybe an excited grandmother-to-be is coming to help and you can hardly wait to see her; maybe she's on her way and you are secretly dubious about how the whole arrangement is going to work out. Maybe one or both of you, the parents, aren't working and time is no problem but money most definitely is; maybe one or both of you are employed and this baby has to time its arrival pretty precisely to fit into the program. More often than not, Murphy's Law seems to be involved in the whole process: if there is a way for something to go wrong, it will. Fortunately, what usually "goes wrong" isn't the baby; it's the logistics.

So, if you're like most of us, you find yourself under way on this parenting business with a baby that you've fallen wholly in love with, but you're surrounded by practical arrangements that have got snarled up somehow (too much family? not enough? a week earlier than you expected? two weeks later than you thought possible?); you're struggling to cope with much less sleep than you're accustomed to, and what you get is broken sleep in any case; and you're in an emotional turmoil because you thought you would handle the whole business calmly and efficiently and instead when the baby cries for hours (which sometimes, unfortunately, they do) you feel like sitting down and bawling along with her. It isn't quite what you had in mind.

It's not that most of us feel like that all the time. The point is that we don't anticipate feeling like that at all. Having children, becoming a family, is part of the eternal plan. I think most of us expect that if we're worthy, we will automatically be up to the challenge. You simply don't expect to feel totally incompetent and overwhelmed by the thousands of little jobs, many of which you haven't done since you stopped baby-sitting (and then your mother or the mother you were sitting for usually had taken care of the major jobs, like laundry and meal preparation).

Part of the problem is that even without realizing it, we arrive at parenthood influenced by all the advertisements and other propaganda that subtly indicates that new parents should be serene and untroubled, existing in a wonder world of comfort and luxury. (Take, for example, the average nursery illustrated in any ad for baby toiletries or disposable diapers.) New mothers, it appears, are slender and perfectly made up and drift about in lace-edged white negligees, cradling a contented baby; new fathers lean against the door frame and look fondly proud. It certainly does make a pretty picture.

Unfortunately, in real life most new mothers are thick-waisted and slack-bellied, with hair doing whatever their hair does when nobody does anything with it, wearing whatever they pulled out of the laundry, which has abruptly mushroomed from a routine weekly job to a continuous imperative, with piles of dirty clothes—the baby's and theirs—and stacks of clean ones that probably won't be put away before they have to be used because the baby's spit up or wet (or worse) all over himself and Mom again. Most fathers are trying to keep their ordinary schedules and do as much as they can to help as well, but not all of them know how to do what their wives need them to do and they're wondering nervously if this is the way things are going to be from now on.

On the really bad days—and we all have some of them—the impulse to somehow get out of all of this, to get back to comfortable, familiar irresponsibility, can surprise us with its strength. But the fact remains that we have to stick to the job. Somebody still has to be the adult, and we're the closest approximation available. We can't get away from the bald fact of an infant's dependency. Whether or not you feel either one of you knows how to be a parent, the two of you are the only parents the baby has, and at too many of the times when you truly feel at your wit's end, only one of you will be there. At those moments, you, in all your unprepared, uncertain singularity, are the parent that baby has. You can hold him as he wails and cry as hard as he does, and when you miserably snuffle to a stop, you have to carry on taking care of him. It's up to you; there's nobody else there.

Even more distressing than the practical problems, however, is the discovery that a lot of other strong emotions come along with the newly discovered love of this new person entrusted to you. We were prepared to be good parents who adore their babies. We knew there were bad parents who do not. What each of us discovers is that we are both a good parent and a bad parent. Sometimes we can hardly bear the sweetness of our love for our babies, and sometimes they make us so unbelievably angry that we frighten ourselves. We can find ourselves wishing with the greatest possible sincerity that we could go back to a life without them.

Particularly with our understanding of the gospel, we're not supposed to feel that way. We're supposed to have matured beyond such selfishness and grown into something closer to Christlike generosity. We're not supposed to resent giving up a separate life of our own: we're supposed to be mothers and fathers in Zion. The discovery that we may not have got anywhere near there yet forces us to come nose-to-nose with our own immaturity.

That's the basic problem, of course. Here we are, just barely adults ourselves—am I the only one to have had the eerie feeling in the early days that what I was really doing was playing house?—and what have we gone and done? We have undertaken permanent earthly responsibility for one of God's children. "Teach me, guide me, walk beside me" sounds just fine when as children we sing it in church. It must have been in the first turbulent days of motherhood that I realized, appalled, it was *me*, as incompetent as I was, that that song was talking about, and I know that what I wanted at that moment was for my mother to come and show me what to do and take over, the way she used to when I was a little girl.

However you happen to react, I suspect what we're all facing at those moments is the realization that we've bitten off more than we can chew without a lot of help, and whereas our idea of help might most logically be that the Lord raise up somebody to cope with everything we feel unsure about (a divine nanny/housekeeper would do well as a start), the Lord's idea of an answer to fervent prayer, in my experience, seems to be a little different. It seems the Lord instead means to use the resources we already have to prune and shape us into capable, accountable adults who can carry the responsibility we've undertaken, often so lightly, and help him bring these fresh new spirits through mortality back to his presence.

The easy way, of course—and I've had times of feeling that it would be a far better method from my children's perspective—would be to outfit each child with a set of perfect parents. Instead, what they seem generally to get is us, a completely miscellaneous set of individuals with idiosyncratic strengths and peculiarities. Just think how much easier my daughters' lives would be if they had a mother who never got cross or was inconsistent or absent-minded! Unfortunately, as my mother points out, the Lord doesn't rely on perfect people for anything, not even running the wards and stakes of Zion. He doesn't have any. He takes what he does have, which is men and women who are stubborn, indecisive, self-righteous, well-intentioned but procrastinate a lot, hot-tempered, phlegmatic, insecure, or domineering; and by throwing us all together and requiring that we work jointly on common projects, the Lord sees that we rub off our rough edges banging against each other and, often, driving each other nuts.

It's out of this same unpromising material that the Lord makes parents for innocent little children, and most of us discover strengths we never knew we possessed.

It's not an easy process. I have always loved C. S. Lewis's adaptation of a parable by George MacDonald that describes the Lord's methods of hauling us toward perfection: "Imagine yourself as a living house. God comes in to rebuild that house. At first, perhaps, you can understand what He is doing. He is getting the drains right and stopping the leaks in the roof and so on: you knew that those jobs needed doing and so you are not surprised. But presently he starts knocking the house about in a way that hurts abominably and does not seem to make sense. What on earth is He up to? The explanation is that He is building quite a different house from the one you thought of—throwing out a new wing here, putting on an extra floor there, running up towers, making courtyards. You thought you were going to be made into a decent little cottage: but He is building a palace." (C. S. Lewis, *Mere Christianity* [New York: Macmillan, 1952], p. 160.)

Of course, the Lord can build palaces—and does—out of people who never have the opportunity of becoming parents, but there's little doubt that the responsibility of being a mother or a father is a fast, high road to learning lessons that most of us would valiantly resist learning any other way. Which of us, after all, really comes to the conclusion that we need to be a bit more patient and then deliberately goes out to find the most exasperating, irritating set of circumstances available just to develop that virtue?

On the other hand, just think of how much patience you are compelled to learn when you, a perfectly average parent, are trying to get the day going but are impeded by a three-year-old who is going to put on her sweater herself the way she has been taught, which involves placing the sweater very carefully on the floor and if you touch it *at all* you get glared at and the sweater has to be repositioned very exactly. Meanwhile, the clock ticks and time passes and you do your best not to go into cardiac arrest. By the time your daughter announces she is ready (at long last having arranged the sweater to her satisfaction and then slowly and with infinite care having put her arms into it and pulled it on over her head), you may be fit to be tied, but if you've managed to resist the temptation to scream and yell and put that sweater on her, like it or not, you've learned a great deal. You've learned that it is possible to keep control of your tongue, that you can, if pressed, reorganize your own priorities to respect the priorities of someone else, even someone as young as three years old, and you are rewarded by your daughter's complacent pleasure in the fact that she did it all by herself. It's unlikely you will have achieved patience—whatever that might mean—in that single episode, but you've made some progress, and, in any case, you're going to get lots of other opportunities for further practical applications. There is, after all, the question of who is going to open the door of the car.

There are obviously a lot of different ways to approach character development, but it seems to me that parenting, as an efficient method of pruning self-indulgence and encouraging patience and self-control and unselfishness (among other virtues), would take a lot of beating. Not that it all happens in a sudden blaze of glory: just as our children seem to need repetition to learn both simple ideas like picking their clothes up off the floor and complicated ones like honesty and compassion, so we seem to need to learn the same lessons over and over again. We think we have learned tolerance of individual differences with our first child and then discover we have to learn it all over again—and differently this time—with the second and third. We have achieved what feels like saintly patience at one stage—a young son's resistance to the concept of regular bathing, for example—and then time works its magic and he turns into a teenager and can't be dislodged from the bathroom without bitter protests, and we have to learn to be patient about that, too.

Sometimes the ways we are being taught to stretch and grow are relatively easy (if irritating on occasion), and we can shrug and share our perplexities and challenges with our friends and even laugh about them a little. Sometimes—particularly when you're struggling to find the wisdom to cope with headstrong rebellion—the gap between what you hoped for and what seems to be happening yawns so widely that you can only confess how much it hurts to the person who shares the heartache and responsibility of parenting with you—or, of course, to the Lord, and sometimes it helps to remember that the child who is breaking your heart is his child as well and that whether you can see how or not, both of you are working on the project.

We struggle to teach our children what we ourselves still need to learn. We preach kindness, knowing that we are too often unkind. We talk about self-control, and unselfishness, and patience—and then we lose our tempers and feel sorry for ourselves and demand instant improvement on everybody else's part but our own.

Our inevitable failures should teach us humility. Unfortunately, if I am in any way typical, sometimes we are too cross to learn. It seems to take failing over and over again before I seem to get around to noticing that it is always the Lord's hand that helps me back up again, that in his love for me, his child, I should be seeing the pattern for my dealings with mine. It seems to take unbelievably long for me to get around to noticing, in fact, how very short of what I need to be I still am, and yet that no matter how cross and irritable I get the Lord still loves me.

It is love, after all, that sustains us through all the rest of it. It is knowing that we have the promise that the flashes of perfect harmony that we achieve here can be wonderfully amplified and extended in eternity that keeps us going when the daily routine seems to be getting out of control. The promise hangs there, luminously bright, whether we remember to look at it or not.

In the meantime, we all stumble along trying to get it right. We have to teach our toddlers not to thump their companions, even if Bobby did snatch the truck, and we have to teach our schoolchildren that not all the words they learn at school are acceptable additions to their vocabulary. We have to teach our adventurous adolescents what curfews are and that they will be enforced. Sometimes our offspring take these lessons agreeably and sometimes they don't; and when I am struggling with their resistance, trying to trust valiantly that somehow this whole process is helping to develop my character as well, I sometimes murmur petulantly, "But how much character do I need?"

And all the time, I know the answer. "More than you've got, honey. More than you've got."

2

Unselfishness

What's Yours Is Yours and What's Mine Is Yours, Too

Unselfishness does not appear to be a virtue that we are inclined to acquire all of our own accord. Being self-centered is the way we all start out, and it takes civilization to teach us the advantages of behaving otherwise. Natural man is naturally selfish; undiluted self-interest is a very powerful element of the survival instinct. Natural man is determined that he is going to survive whether or not anyone else does.

We see a shadow of that in our sweet, dear little babies, who howsoever sweet or dear have absolutely no concern in the middle of the night (or any other time) for whether or not their exhausted mothers have been up four times already and are so tired they're seeing double. If a baby is hungry or uncomfortable, a baby howls until somebody comes and does something about it. It takes quite a long time before the baby is capable of taking anything but his own needs into consideration and begins to learn that sometimes he has to wait for what he wants.

Some get as far as fully grown adulthood and seem never to have grasped the concept. When they're little, we call those who stubbornly insist on their own needs being tended first "spoiled." Later on, we say they're rude or egocentric or male chauvinist pigs (if they're male) or use a number of other descriptive phrases, some of which are polite and many of which are not. We all encounter these folks here and there: the woman who bulls through the supermarket express line with too many items and makes such a fuss if challenged that it's just easier to let her go through than to hold everybody else up even longer arguing about it; the driver who cuts from lane to lane, paying no attention to anybody behind or beside him, and leaves all the responsibility for avoiding a collision to the other drivers; those obnoxious creeps who push their way into the head of any line, apparently on the principle that, unlike the rest of us, they don't have the time to wait around. "Stupid jerks," I find myself muttering. "Badly brought up."

So how do we, paragons that we are, who are *always* courteous and considerate and have never cut in front of anybody else in traffic, get to be so wonderful? Or, to be somewhat more realistic, so nearly wonderful?

Well, we certainly started out being just as piggy as anyone else, and when we're tired or cross or not feeling particularly well, we can probably pig right along with the best of them still. Ideally, however, we learn at a reasonably early stage that although getting what we want when we want it is obviously satisfying, being rewarded by smiles and hugs and general approval for being willing to wait around a little can be very satisfying, too. Infants may be egocentric, but they are also eager to please, and they can be led by love, which is the threshold for teaching.

Certainly love seems to be the only effective way to come to true unselfishness. Oh, I suppose it's possible to learn the types of behavior which we think of as un-selfish—showing consideration for other people, sharing possessions, giving up something that you wanted for somebody else's sake—simply as politeness or common courtesy, and indeed most of the principles of what we grandly call etiquette are nothing more than the outward flourishes of unselfishness. But if we're serious about the business of acquiring unselfishness as a part of what we most essentially are, the outward flourishes have to be accompanied by a genuine reshaping of the natural man, so that instead of thinking, "I am doing this for you be-cause you will think better of me, which will be to my ad-vantage in the long run," we are spontaneously thinking, "I am doing this for you because I care for you."

To get *there* takes love.

When the Pharisees were trying to get Jesus to entangle himself in his own teachings, they demanded of him which commandment was the "great commandment" in the law. He told them that the first, great commandment was that we should love the Lord our God. And then he added that the second commandment was "like unto it." We were to love our neighbors as ourselves. (Matthew 22:36–39.) That seems to have temporarily silenced the Pharisees, who couldn't find anything about that to argue with, although one gathers that most of them honored the commandment more in theory than in practice. When a lawyer challenged Jesus at another time to define for him who would be his neighbor, Jesus told him the parable of the Good Samaritan, which basically boils down to the principle that whoever you see in need is your neighbor, whether or not the two of you live anywhere near each other or even have a common cultural background (see Luke 10:29–37). If we stick to just loving the people who love us, Jesus pointed out, what reward do we expect for that? Even the tax gatherers (a class of people who often collected on their own behalf as well as the state's and therefore were viewed with justifiable suspicion at the time) love people who love them. (See Matthew 5:46.)

So as disciples of Christ, we're expected to get beyond

the elementary stage of loving our nearest and dearest. Still, it's a place to start, and in fact it's the place where most of us do start. We grow from infancy to childhood, from loving ourselves to loving the people who take care of us, and we begin to discover that doing things for other people makes them happy and that that makes us happy. If we can't remember the early stages of learning those lessons ourselves, we are reminded of them when we see a small child with his face lit up because he is bringing the newspaper in for his mother or father, or the concentration of a little girl who (loving cookies herself) has carefully placed the two biggest cookies on a plate and is carrying them into the room where her parents are watching television. When these earliest seedlings of unselfishness are rewarded with appreciation and approval, the roots flourish and go deep.

Sometimes the object of our beginning efforts at unselfishness isn't even human. A lot of us learn important lessons about unselfishness when we undertake care of a pet. Playing with a cat or dog is fun, but we discover inevitably that they get hungry at the hours when they're used to being fed, even if we aren't thinking about them at the time and happen to be in the middle of doing something fascinating somewhere else. For most of us, there is at least one episode of finding good old faithful Frisky (or maybe it's the kitten you named Susan) waiting forlornly by an empty bowl because you forgot. Sometimes Frisky or Susan get forgotten more than once or twice before you start being reliable about remembering— or if you have the kind of mother who loves animals on her own account, the animal gets fed, but when you do show up you get treated to a heart-twisting description of what it would be like to love and trust somebody and wait and wait and wait for them to come, which always made me feel like a worm, especially since the animal in question was invariably more forgiving than my mother thought it had any reason to be. It was not my favorite way to learn, but it apparently worked, because now, having nobly fed the pets myself, I deliver a remarkably similar sermon to my children when they come trolling in sometime later, carefree and totally oblivious to the needs of the animals they claim to adore the rest of the time.

Still, I really think the first time we truly begin to learn about spontaneous unselfishness is when we first fall in love—really in love, as opposed to having crushes on this person for fifteen minutes and that person for as much as an hour and a half straight. Honest, genuine love comes as a revelation to us all. Suddenly there is somebody we care about more than we care about ourselves, and the whole experience is illuminated with the excitement and drama of romance. No wonder there are so many songs and stories about it: love is absolutely amazing. There is the wonder of sharing experiences and emotions that you never thought anyone else would understand. There is the excitement of being together, the joy of pleasing, and the delicious discovery that the person you love wants to please you, too.

Under those circumstances, unselfishness is a piece of cake. It's perfectly natural to think of the other person first before you think of yourself. You want what the person you love wants simply and beautifully in the early stages. (The later stages of maturing love are all about weaving together what you each want separately into the fabric of what you want jointly; and one of the facts of growing in love, as opposed to falling in love in the first place, is that both of you will inevitably have loose threads left over, and there are places where the fabric gets kind of wonky. That's why marriages are meant to last for a lifetime and longer: it gives you time to sort that kind of thing out.)

When we have our children, we love them a lot, too, but that love comes in different shapes. Ideally, romantic love that grows into lifetime love between a man and a woman is symmetrical. Each of you bends toward the other. Parental love is a lot of things, but symmetrical it isn't. For a very long time, parental love involves pouring yourself out generously day after day (and night after night) and getting very little in return except the satisfaction of giving.

Even long after your child has grown past infancy, you will be engaged in what on bad days seems like pretty thankless sacrifice. After all, the old cliche of the parent snapping, "Is this all the thanks I get?" is a cliche precisely because so many parents have said exactly that.

It's not surprising that this sacrifice doesn't always come easily. It's not that we don't love the children; we do. But there are those down days when it seems a million years since anybody thought about *you* first. It's always the baby first. You know you're not supposed to feel that way, but you do. Well, I guess the beginnings of parental unselfishness come when you feel grumpy and hard done by and you still put aside what you'd like to be doing and get back to the job of being a parent. Rejoicing in it may come later: one step at a time.

Parenthood is one big blooming opportunity for unselfishness. Obviously the Lord means us to learn by doing, but instead of letting us practice little bits of unselfishness here and there, he tosses us directly into the deep end and clearly expects us not only to stay afloat ourselves but to keep the small person entrusted to us afloat as well.

The toss into the deep end begins even before the arrival of the child. Having myself acquired children both by birth and adoption, I am in a position to testify that both methods require the prospective parent to exhibit a whole lot more unselfishness than he or she is likely to possess at that stage. The acquisition methods may be different, but they are equally trying.

When a woman is engaged in the homemade version of child production, she gets started practicing unselfishness right at the beginning. Her first suspicions that a baby might be on the way are probably simultaneous with the overwhelming urge to start out the bright new day by throwing up. I have read a theory somewhere that morning sickness (or evening sickness, or all-day-long sickness if you're particularly unfortunate) is nature's mechanism to keep pregnant women from ingesting foods that might be harmful to the baby. If that's true, I can't help wondering why a less unpleasant method couldn't have been worked out. I loathe and detest throwing up under any circumstances and always have. But I was excited about having a baby and could hardly wait to have one, and so if in order to have a baby I had to feel like throwing up for a few months, I guess I was prepared to throw up. The first lessons on putting my baby first and myself second had begun.

That's just for starters. Long before there is a bulge or the first flutter of movement, mothers-to-be discover somebody else has to be taken into account in what have always been purely personal issues. You're used to vigorous physical activity? You can't decide that all by yourself now; it's probably okay, but check with the doctor. It's springtime, and whatever it is that makes you sneeze and your nose run is in full irritating flower? You may know exactly what to take for it, but this time you can't take it without making sure it won't harm the baby. You can't take anything, in fact, without clearing it first. Suddenly everything that goes into your mouth has to be rethought in terms of the interests of something so small you can't even tell it's there. Hooray for the baby, you think, as you sneeze and blow.

After a while, of course, it becomes quite obvious that somebody else is there, too. Clothes have always been important to you and you've been secretly proud of your trim shape? Well, your shape will return eventually, but in the meantime your waist is nonexistent and the stylishness of any clothes you wear is modified by the necessity to accommodate a gradually enlarging midsection that eventually looks as if you had strapped a watermelon around your belly. Your sleep is interrupted by vigorous internal activity that you didn't start and can't stop—and of course the bigger and the stronger the baby gets inside, the more aware you become that at term it is going to have to get out one way or another.

Pre-adoptive "pregnancy" lacks the physical trials but offers a whole different set of emotional ones. Practically nobody starts out with the idea of adopting; usually the decision to apply follows the barren emptiness of infertility, which feels like failure even if the world around us makes it amply obvious on a daily basis that the ability to procreate has nothing to do with virtue or personal worthiness. Still, there it is: the haunting sense of "Why aren't we good enough?"

Medical investigation of infertility (quite apart from the flood of helpful advice from well-meaning relatives and friends) is not something that most of us would choose to do as a form of recreation. You answer questions that you don't feel are anybody else's business, and what you would rather have be romantic and exciting becomes programmed and clinical—all for the sake of a child that may never come to be. You have to grow into unselfishness for a hope and a prayer and a will-o'-the-wisp.

One way and another, by the time you get around to filling out the forms for adoption, you've already done a fair bit of rearrangement of your personal priorities to make space for this child you so passionately desire. Then comes the indignity of dealing with somebody else (who may or may not be wise and kind) who has the right to poke through that rearrangement and come to a conclusion as to whether it's been done properly or not. There are more questions; inspections of your affairs, your home; inquisitions into what your friends and your employers think of you. Through the whole affair it's made perfectly clear that if there were a pyramid representing this process, your interests as would-be adoptive parents would be right at the bottom. Above you come the interests of the natural mother (increasingly including the father as well, whatever his relationship to the mother), and above that come the interests of the baby— and unselfishness demands that you accept and understand that as true. After all, the baby should have the chance to go to the most secure and loving home available, and, as you can't help knowing even if they don't remind you frequently, there are lots of other fine families who would be overjoyed to adopt if you fall short. It adds a nasty zing to the whole trauma of hoping to be chosen.

No matter how you do it, the acquisition of a child involves labor, whether it be physical or emotional. Nor is all the work done by women: prospective fathers begin similar adjustments even before actual parenthood. There is the looming inevitability of sharing his wife with someone else, as well as the discovery that what is probably the reasonably new freedom of adulthood is about to be cramped to a reasonably substantial degree. There are new obligations, new priorities, and, without a doubt, new expenses. Most of all, there's the uncertainty: what is this new life as a parent really going to be like?

Then the children come and we find out.

Everybody knows about the ordinary, run-of-the-mill ways in which we sacrifice for our children. We walk endlessly through the dark hours of early colicky nights, trying to ease a wailing infant into rest. We drop what we're doing to listen carefully to the small person tugging at our elbow, even if what she wants to tell us is a lengthy recap of the plotline of a cartoon that was pretty lame even if you could see the pictures. We spend hours drilling on spelling lists, puzzling out arithmetic story problems, and trying to figure out what the science teacher means them to be doing in that assignment anyway. We sit in docile rows for school activities and try to volunteer when we're needed, whether it's really convenient or not. Little children, little problems; big children, big problems: as they get older, we struggle to draw the difficult line between what are the matters of little consequence and not worth arguing about and what are the critical issues that require us to protect them against their own immature bad judgment while they are growing into the full scope of their free agency. Accompanying the off-again, on-again rumbles of confrontation, the music that resounds through the house is increasingly often their music, the program on TV what they want to watch. And over and over and over through the years, when those choices have to be made as to what we can buy, what the children need or want is likely to come well ahead of what we would have, left to ourselves.

27

All those are the outside manifestations, the things everybody sees. What we can't know before we get into parenthood is the quiet internal revolution. It's as if you've grown invisible new limbs: you used to be able to dash off, free as a bird, and now there is always awareness of the children, an awareness as much attached to you as your arms or legs. The fact of your responsibility is forever bubbling around somewhere in the back of your consciousness. They are always there in your waking hours, and you find yourself dreaming about them at night. In the early days, before you get used to it, even on what should be a carefree evening out you find yourself dashing to the phone to check that the substitute caretaker is caretaking properly. Much later on, when cars get involved, you may be getting on with what you're supposed to be doing, but there's a vague sense of anxiety that surfaces with increasing frequency until you hear the reassuring crunch of the tires on the driveway again. In between, in the middle of the night you rouse to faint sounds that might have never wakened you before, and during the day you discover you can locate your adventurous son who disappeared into a crowd at the zoo by the glimpse of as little as a square inch of the back of his head.

You worry about the darn kids even when everything's fine. You fuss about whether they suck their thumbs, whether their teeth are straight, whether they are shorter than the average or awkwardly tall, whether their hair lies down limply or sticks straight up, and whether they need glasses. In a funny way, it's almost as if your vanity is transferred to them: you used to worry about what people thought about the way *you* look, and now you worry what people think about their appearance and whether anybody but you will notice the spot on the shirt (what on earth did she find to eat that she could have spilled there anyway?).

When they do something splendid, you are so proud you could pop. You tell all the good true friends and relatives that are handy and find yourself embarrassingly inclined to brag to anyone else that happens to be available. When they have disappointments that desolate them, you are in anguish. That kind of identification, although it makes the sacrificing easier, isn't really what we anticipate before we get into the web of parenthood.

Naturally, as the number of children we have increases, so do the opportunities for unselfishness. In fact, the opportunities for unselfishness multiply to the point where, as a simple matter of self-preservation, we have to start drawing lines—lines which in the long run are not a bad thing for the children themselves, since in the complicated web of family interactions, everybody can't have everything they individually want and do everything they would individually choose to do all the time. The needs and choices have to be interwoven. Sometimes it's Susan's turn to be the princess for the day (or the hour); sometimes it's Bobby's activities that take precedence over everybody else's—he's involved in a soccer tournament, for instance, and everything else stops while he's being ferried back and forth and the family is commandeered to become loyal cheerleaders on the sidelines until the bittersweet game when his team loses, and although you feel for his disappointment, you still are aware of a small squeak of rejoicing that you finally get to do something else with your life.

In fact, since very few of us get turned into truly noble creatures by the mere fact of parenthood, the truth is that we all have times when we get fed up with the new order of things being them first and us sometime in the future if at all. There are definitely the days when we simply flatly rebel against endlessly reorganizing our lives to accommodate theirs, and if things are getting out of whack, that may not be an entirely bad thing. After all, there are differences between being unselfish and being a doormat.

Some things, of course, are open and shut cases. By taking on a child, we take on the obligation to make sure that child is fed and clothed, sheltered and given enough love and instruction so that both his mind and his spirit can grow. Those are non-negotiable items; we can't decide we just don't feel up to supplying any of those today, which is what leads mothers (and sometimes fathers), coughing and shivering with a feverish cold, to haul themselves out of bed to slap together a peanut butter sandwich so that the preschooler who has been parked in front of the television all morning gets something to eat for lunch. Small children have to be fed, and if you're the only one there, you have to do the feeding. But that's not to say that it's equally obligatory to haul yourself out of bed to change the channel at half-hour intervals. Nor, in other contexts, does the new pair of shoes always have to be for somebody else, or the music lessons be only for the children. If you have limited finances, and you passionately want to learn to play the piano and the children couldn't care less, it's kind of dumb to relentlessly sacrifice yourself on the altar of their lack of enthusiasm.

It seems to me that in some ways it's worse than dumb. Surely one of the worst things any child can grow up believing is that he or she is the logical center of the universe. One of the great strengths of the gospel is that it teaches us firmly that each of us is individual and distinct, with free agency and the potential for divinity within us. That's a wonderfully encouraging promise for me, but with it comes the reality that everybody else has the same promise. The only way I can distinguish myself in the eyes of the Lord is by my righteous choices and my obedience to his principles. Apart from that, we are none of us grander than anyone else. We all have different gifts, and those bring different responsibilities. I suppose we all have times of thinking that somebody else's gifts might be nicer to have, but those choices were not given to us. The consolation is that nobody's gifts entitle him or her to take center stage in singular splendor.

It sometimes seems that children learn the lessons we don't mean to teach them faster than the ones we do. If day in, day out we demonstrate by catering to their every whim that our wishes and desires are of little consequence compared to theirs, most children leap to the conclusion that they are important enough to disregard anyone else as well. This is not exactly a healthy attitude to set out with. For one thing, if we don't teach our children that they have to accommodate themselves to others, the world will, but the world's lessons are likely to be a lot rougher.

Nor is giving children an inflated sense of self-importance good for us. There is no doubt that in the equation of parent and child, the weight of service flows to the child, but it is nonetheless an equation, and we do come into it. Sometimes what we get is the satisfaction of giving (and it's usually parenthood that teaches us most joyfully how rich that satisfaction can be); and sometimes what we get is the love and trust that our children give back to us; and sometimes I suspect what we get is the absolute delight of temporarily shedding the responsibility and doing exactly what we individually and personally want to do—which we would never relish one-tenth as much if we got to do it every day of the week. Rarity hath its own charms.

Besides, the unselfishness we are forced into acquiring in the course of parenting isn't meant to stop there. Sometimes, sadly, it does: haven't we all encountered the parents who will do anything for their own child but jealously measure out any gesture of generosity to anyone else? In those cases, I suspect that what's going on with the parent is not so much unselfishness toward the child as so incorporating the child into the parent's own ego that doing for the child is really nothing more than another way of doing for him or herself.

Unselfishness is meant to be liberating. By stepping out of the tight circle of what's right for us, or what we want to do, or what we want to have, we get to move out to the wider world beyond our own boundaries. For one thing, the unselfishness that we practice, willy-nilly, with our children should enlarge the possibilities of our marriages.

There are a dozen ways a day we can serve each other, and do. Moms home with the children know well that wonderful hour when the day is winding down and the children are hungry and fractious, and Mom has been a good mom all day and is tired, too, and dinner has to be fixed, and the children want to play underfoot or lean against the back of her legs and whine or, as alternative entertainment, engage in loud, pointless squabbling and then shove each other out of the way in their haste to come tattle. Dad gets home at the end of *his* long day with its own particular difficulties and frustrations, looking forward to a chance to unwind, and opens the door to discover he has entered a tank of barracudas. Ah, home sweet home.

So what happens then? Well, this being the real world, I expect sometimes, just as at my house, things deteriorate from there. Everybody gets cross and silent or cross and loud, but either way everyone feels aggrieved. Eventually dinner gets on the table and eaten, more or less, and then in the general bustle of baths and stories (if everybody hasn't gotten *too* cross) and tucking into bed and peace finally descending, apologetic overtures, if not exactly apologies, mellow the atmosphere enough so that Mom and Dad eventually collapse into bed themselves feeling reasonably friendly and resolving individually to handle the whole thing better in the future, but hoping it doesn't all happen again tomorrow at least.

The good days are the days when Dad opens the door to the barracudas and he and Mom look at each other and whichever one's feeling marginally less badgered (as long as it isn't always the same one) takes a deep breath and, using the unselfishness capacity which has been so richly developed with the children thus far, taps into the current of love that is always there and somehow makes a bit of space for the other one, providing the lubrication of devotion for the rough spots. Maybe it's Dad unhitching the children so that Mom can concentrate on just getting dinner on the table in relative peace and quiet; maybe it's Mom keeping the kids with her and out of the bedroom so that Dad can change his clothes and get himself together for a few undisturbed minutes before he steps back into his family responsibilities. Whichever way it happens doesn't matter, as long as it goes both ways in the long run. The unselfishness, growing out of and enriched by their love, soothes and revives both of them.

It would be wonderful if all of us were capable of rising to those heights all the time, but we're still learning. As long as we're reaching, the days when it does happen are enough to keep us going. Hopefully, the good days give us enough of a bounce to be able to reach beyond our own family circle to the larger family of man around us. We have neighbors who live next door and across the street and neighbors we have only bumped into in passing. There are good people (and not-so-good people) in near and distant places who need our time and our energy and our love expressed in both. What was it Jesus told us about the publicans who just loved the people who loved them back?

Most of what is recorded from Jesus' time on earth is his public life, but from that public life there's a lot to learn that applies to our private lives. I wonder if Jesus ever had moments of being exasperated with his disciples, the way I get exasperated with my children. They grew into great men, true Apostles of the Lord (as the book of Acts testifies), but they started out (as the Gospels show) as perfectly ordinary people, much like us. Remember their arguing about who was the greatest among them? Remember the way they fell asleep during Jesus' agonizing vigil in Gethsemane? It was late and they were tired—the way you and I get tired—and I guess none of them recognized Christ's anguish. After all, he was their Lord, and I don't suppose it seemed possible to them that anything really bad could happen to him. I've even heard it argued that Judas betrayed Jesus only because he figured Jesus would always escape miraculously (remember how often he had melted into the crowd and away from sticky situations?) and that way the disciples would have their Christ and the thirty pieces of silver as well, and he, being keeper of the purse, knew they could always use the money. Remember how Peter—who grew into a man of authority and wisdom and boundless courage—was frightened into denying that he knew anything about Jesus three times, how Thomas had to see with his own eyes before he would believe: they started out as simple, uneducated fishermen, most of them. But was Christ ever cross with them? He taught simply, patiently, lovingly—a pattern for us to hold up before us as we take on our own daily challenges, dealing with people around us who are sometimes obstinate, or cynical, or slow.

The unselfishness we learn from Christ's example and from the necessities of being a parent teach us the ways of weaving an eternal family together, where priorities are always changing (and presumably always will be) and where what is needed from us mutates from minute to minute. Beset by the most ordinary hassles and frustrations, we struggle to learn how to find the balance between what we want and what the others need, and through the experience of giving ourselves lavishly (even if we didn't really anticipate how much would be required), we discover an eternal principle: the deeper the space we hollow out with daily routine unselfishness and with repeatedly sacrificing what seems easiest and most convenient at the moment, the more room there is to accommodate the love.

And suddenly, maybe when you got dragged out to the backyard to play catch with a son (when what you really had had in mind was peacefully watching television or washing your hair), that love catches up with you. You didn't mean to enjoy yourself, but the ball sails back and forth; you're both laughing and lunging to catch it, and in the middle of a perfectly ordinary backyard, you get a glimpse of what forever will be like.

It's enough to keep you going.

3

Tolerance

Not Only Coats
Have Many Colors

Unselfishness is all very well and good. As we grew up, we all came to know about unselfishness. We knew (uneasily) that our parents were rising to heights of unselfishness from time to time while coping with us and our requirements, and so the idea that we would be required to develop similarly for our children was certainly no great shock.

Tolerance is something different. I don't know that I expected to need tolerance in dealing with my children. I think before I had children I was of the opinion that tolerance was a fine civic virtue (which it is) and never expected it to get closer to me than what was required to be a good citizen and a good neighbor.

Tolerance, after all, has everything to do with differences. You don't need tolerance when you aren't confronted by anything that is unfamiliar or makes you uncomfortable. If everybody had an obsessive enthusiasm for order, neatniks would have no need for tolerance to get along with those who believe there's a place for everything, all right, but everything goes in the same place—a nice untidy pile. If everybody's musical passion was for the classics, or even folk music, nobody would ever have to learn tolerance for rock, whether alternative, soft, hard, or rap—although they still might have a word or two to say about volume, and lyrics. If everybody had skin exactly the same color (maybe a nice nondescript gray), nobody would have to teach racial tolerance, because there could be no distinctions built on skin pigmentation—which, when you think about it, is an odd thing to get fixated on. We seem to be able to adjust to differences in eye color without much fuss. If we were all raised in a universal homogeneous culture, with only one set of traditions passed on, there would be no need for cultural tolerance (and presumably no ethnic warfare, either), but the price would be the terrible one of living in a world with no individualistic quirks and none of the fascination of discovering different people who speak a different language and eat different foods and have their own traditional wisdom and art. It would, in fact, probably be much like the world that Satan envisioned, with no choices and no glory for anyone but Satan and nothing unexpected ever, ever happening.

Fortunately, we don't live in the world Satan proposed. We live in a world alive with all the possibilities of free agency—bristling with color and vibrancy and tradition and dozens of different ways of doing the same things—and one of our jobs here is to learn to be flexible and tolerant enough so that all of us, so richly and wonderfully different, can get along with each other peaceably and harmoniously and only teach each other lessons of love.

That's the theory, and as long as the theory stays at arm's length, most of us can adjust to it fine. Being tolerant of the outsiders living on somebody else's block is usually no big problem. The difficulties start when the outsiders move in next door to you, or worse yet, turn up right at home and turn out to be your very own children. We're not really prepared to discover that our children might have a different way of looking at or reacting to the world than we do. We might not have thought about it much, but it just seemed logical that our children would grow up having the same general kinds of responses to experience that we did—earning the beads and pins in Cub Scouts maybe, or learning to knit long, lumpy scarves, or telling each other scary stories at Halloween—and instead, sometimes it seems to be coming out all different. It's not just a matter of circumstances, such as the fact that they have computers in school and we didn't. It's something more fundamental. As much as we want to share good times like the ones we had and help our children over bad times like the ones we endured back then, it can't be done. With some children it's more obvious than with others, but the bottom line is that they are their own people. They aren't going to relive the childhood we remember.

Maybe you were a tomboy who loved sports, and your daughter wants to sit home and play with her Barbies. Maybe you spent your formative years trying valiantly to hide your terror of heights and roller coasters and the bully down the block, and your son is bluff and husky and swaggering and seems uncomfortably like the boys who scared the living daylights out of you all those years ago. Or maybe the differences between the two of you are subtle and fleeting and troubling only when you reach out to say comfortingly, "I know just how you're feeling," and your child, bone of your bone, flesh of your flesh, looks back at you and it takes no genius to figure out what he's thinking: *You don't have the vaguest idea.*

It's not that we expect to rear clones. Any fool can look at the collection of babies in the average hospital nursery and see that they come in all shapes and sizes and, even in the first forty-eight hours, temperaments. There are babies who are big and sturdy and some who are small and frail. Some are dopey and dozy and some are wide awake, checking out the new environment. Some bellow and some whimper. You stare at your own baby with wonder and excitement, speculating on what is going on behind that crumpled face. Do you recognize each other somehow? Maybe. Your baby is likely to have a lot of you in her—heredity plays its part in us all, but not always the part we expect. Heredity plays funny tricks.

What we notice first, of course, is what heredity does to the outside. There are those who claim all new babies look like Winston Churchill, but your new baby is also likely to resemble grandparents (on both sides), Uncle Heber, Aunt Alta, Great-aunt Julia, your brother-in-law, Mom, Dad, an older sister, or some distant relative that you've never laid eyes on but, according to your mother, had hair growing just like that. Still, it isn't usually the outside that gives us pause for thought. It's what we discover about the inside as the months grow into years and our children grow into their own individuality.

Maybe an obliging infant who looked just exactly like her father grows up to share virtually none of his personality traits. Maybe she even shows a distressing tendency to whine, which is the one thing that has always driven her father absolutely crazy. He cannot abide a whining child and here he has one whining on a daily basis in his very own house. Well, clearly she is going to be encouraged strongly to develop a different method of coping with dissatisfaction, but while she's in the learning stages (which inevitably involve relapses), Dad gets to practice sympathy or patience with practices not necessarily in harmony with his own, which is a long way of saying tolerance. Unless he has the energy and perseverance to make a big deal out of every single occurrence, he is going to have to practice tolerance for the learning curve.

There are less clear-cut issues than whining, of course. Few of us are really enthusiastic about little voices that go on and on and on (nasally), although not all of us go ballistic about it. But what about the insistently extroverted child who exults in being the life of the party—any party, even the checkout line in the grocery store? There's nothing inherently wrong with having high spirits and holding center stage, but if that child happens to have been born to a dear shy and retiring couple whose greatest dread is being conspicuous, the process of getting used to each other can take a lot out of all of them.

What does tolerance demand of us?

Maybe we'd better start out by considering what we're *not* asked to tolerate. Sin, for one thing. The Lord doesn't: as Alma told Helaman and his other sons, "The Lord cannot look upon sin with the least degree of allowance" (Alma 45:16). But how often is the problem troubling us really a matter of sin? Obviously sin can be an issue: as our children grow older, it's perfectly possible for them to make choices that we cannot condone. Recognizing that they are spirits entrusted to us for guidance, we do have the obligation to teach and guide them by the principles that we know to be true.

Still, most of the time what's irritating and annoying us isn't really sin per se. Maybe what's worrying us is the old camel's-nose-under-the-tent principle—let in the nose and the rest will inevitably follow. Well, there's truth to that, but there's also the possibility that the camel doesn't have his nose anywhere near the tent yet and in fact is just wandering past. Just seeing anything like the camel anywhere in the area (are we maybe talking about bright purple nail polish here, when you have always been convinced that ladies wear none or the palest pink?) and some of us start jumping up and down and carrying on while our children stare at us with wonder and dismay and, sometimes, with the growing determination not only to lay their hands on the brightest purple available, but to figure out something *really* outrageous, if we're going to get so uptight anyway. Inappropriate parental outrage is not only wearing on the parent, it's too often just plain counterproductive.

Generally, if we're going to take an unyielding stand on our principles, it's just as well to make sure in the first place that what's in fact causing the difficulty is a matter of principle and not simply a fuss about preferences. If, as is so often the case, what we're battling about is a preference, there's no reason why we should expect our children to be governed by what we prefer, however much we wish they would. As far as we know, personal worthiness is not determined solely by length of hair in high school. Both Democrats and Republicans have been known to hold temple recommends. Even girls who wear an astounding amount of eye makeup as an announcement of puberty grow up and become fine mothers in Zion. Maybe what we're fighting about here is not so much the choices they're making as it is about their right to make them.

Tolerance means keeping big issues and little issues distinct. Tolerance means looking at people, even people as close and dear to you as your very own children, and giving them room to be different without your hassling them about it.

Why *do* we get so uptight about trivia? Families have collisions of will about hair color and the advisability of wearing coats on cold days and whether it improves moral fiber to get out of bed at a reasonable hour on a Saturday even if there isn't any specific reason for being up at a particular time. Having gotten involved in disputes on all those issues, I can report, having thought it all over calmly and coolly when I was *not* arguing about it, that hair grows and inevitably returns to whatever color you started out with (and if the return involves a period of coping with orange hair, it is unnecessary to point that out to the orange-haired one and I ought to remember that); that I'm not the one wandering around coatless in a whipping chill wind and hugging myself to keep warm and maybe it takes an episode or two of getting frozen to the bone to decide to bring something warm with you when you go out, even if it's not the coat we were initially fighting about; and that my child's sleeping as late as possible may annoy the living daylights out of me as I do my Saturday chores and errands, but as long as the sleeper's chores get completed sometime that day, it's no skin off my nose if he or she misses a beautiful sunny afternoon doing the assigned inside jobs. Besides which, in all truth, I know that carefree adolescence inevitably gives way to adulthood and responsibility, and the same daughter who is now sleeping blissfully until eleven or later may be up at five tending babies soon enough—too soon, really.

Sometimes our differences are subtle and slippery, and in calm moments you wonder who's being taught tolerance of what. For example, it has taken a friend of mine years to realize that her major problem in dealing with her daughter is that her daughter has inherited her father's phlegmatic temperament. My friend is one of those who lose their tempers swiftly and forget about it as fast; once she has exploded, the whole incident is over and done with, as far as she's concerned. Her husband is slow to anger, but once aroused, it takes him a while to settle down, which has made for interesting matrimonial experiences on occasion. As it has turned out, like father, like daughter. This leads directly to everyday domestic scenarios like this: mother arrives in daughter's room carrying an armload of neatly folded laundry. Daughter is sitting on the floor talking on the telephone, surrounded by casually discarded clothes and other incidentals. Mother reaches full boil in fifteen seconds flat, demands that daughter hang up telephone instantly and commence cleanup, delivers theatrical predictions (complete with agitated arm-waving) of horrific future awaiting daughter if she carries on in this slothful fashion, and slams out of the room bristling with righteous indignation. Five minutes later mother is humming happily while she fishes in the refrigerator for the ingredients for dinner; daughter is up in her room seething, picking up one item at a time from the floor with deliberate fury and muttering to herself. The next day daughter is still aggrieved, and mother is astonished and, having forgotten the whole episode, can't imagine what her daughter's problem might be. According to daughter, mother made a big deal out of nothing the way she always does. According to mother, daughter is sulky, disrespectful, and being thoroughly unpleasant for no apparent reason.

Now, there is no doubt that parenting (or being the child, as far as that goes) in such a situation would be a lot easier if both were working on the same length of fuse. Either they could both be the kind that boil over—which would be noisier, but they would both rise to the drama and take advantage of the emotional release of a short, sharp encounter—or they could both be the kind that just simmer for a while and eventually, with well-developed mutual exasperation, come to a working agreement based on much that isn't ever precisely stated but is communicated nonetheless. However, since the Lord is obviously determined that both of them should grow and develop their capacities for mutual understanding whether it's easy or not, they will probably find themselves facing the same problem over and over again until they learn to solve it properly. In the aforementioned case, that probably involves one of them learning to count to ten and give some warning before erupting and the other learning to speak up about her side of the argument instead of just brooding about it.

Parenting forces us to come to terms with temperamental differences. Of course, you could always say the kids should be forced to as well, but the kids can always come to the easy conclusion that we're nuts and go back to thinking about something else. They don't carry the responsibility; we do. Not all of us face the difficulties of coping with a child whose responses feel alien to us, but all of us have to drive our hearts to understanding.

If, as the gospel teaches us, we are born without memory of our premortal existence, it makes sense that there is a lot about life that we have forgotten or don't understand from our mortal perspective. We can only guess why some things happen as they do, but it seems reasonable to speculate that the Lord has sent each of us the children who can teach us what we individually and uniquely need to learn from our experience on this earth.

Some of the lessons might be obvious ones, and some aren't. Maybe what we need to learn is patience with a stubborn child, maybe that there is something to be said for spontaneity by coping with a child who resists any form of regimentation. Maybe it's discovering that you *can* race to catch up with your child's quick mind that so easily runs circles around your slower responses; maybe it's the humility of recognizing that the child who's struggling academically has skills in dealing with people that you haven't come close to mastering.

Sometimes, locked in misunderstanding and frustration with our exasperating children, we may even begin to despair that we will ever figure out what it was that we needed to know. Why does it have to be so hard? In the manuals and the filmstrips and, as far as we can see, the other families around us, family tranquility comes easily. Well, maybe sometimes it does. But as long as we remain in there, groping for the way to reach each other, we are learning a lot about love and patience and different ways of approaching problems. Maybe we're learning that we don't have all the answers, and hopefully the children are learning that we do have some of them. Maybe those are the lessons we needed to learn.

Maybe, in the worlds and times to come, we will have the satisfaction of sitting down together to evaluate the process when the whole struggle is long behind us. Looking back at mortality with wonder and an entirely different perspective, we might then be able to see how we were hammered into something a little closer to perfection by our head-to-head encounters here. It would indeed be comforting to know that now for sure, but certainty is not one of the gifts we have been given. In dealing with our children—as with so many other aspects of our lives here away from home—we walk by faith.

Tolerance has everything to do with free agency: free agency and the flexibility to accommodate it. Naturally it's hard to be flexible about the ordinary day-by-day routines that we like done the way we want them done, which is of course the most understandable, reasonable, *sensible* way to do them. If we are blessed with children who are comfortable in our patterns, we are blessed indeed. Unfortunately, so many children seem to use their creativity (and their free agency) to figure out a dozen other ways to do whatever it is, or to avoid doing it altogether. The trick is to restrain ourselves from using up quantities of emotional capital unnecessarily. Does it really make any difference in the long run if Jody procrastinates getting down to ironing, in spite of your repeated reminders, until one day she has only a crumpled shirt to wear to school? Maybe that will bother her enough to get herself organized (which was why you assigned her ironing to her in the first place), but maybe she won't be troubled at all. Maybe she will wind up being one of those people who get organized only enough to shake things out briskly as they come out of the dryer (and given the fabrics of today, you'd be hard-pressed to say who does and who doesn't), and that will suit her fine. As an exercise in free agency, it's the kind of morally neutral decision that makes us individuals instead of indistinguishable ciphers—but mothers and daughters still fight about it.

Giving space to free agency means giving up control. As parents, we're likely to have stronger feelings about control than we recognize. It's so much more comfortable to be in control, to have your own hands on the wheel so you can keep on top of where things are going. It's scarier to sit in the passenger seat and watch. Even so, as parents it's our job to gradually let loose of the wheel and slide over to let the young driver try. They have to learn. We have to learn to let go.

One of the lessons we learn on the way to acquiring tolerance is the magnificence of our Heavenly Father's plan. Not only did he keep us free from the kind of control Satan proposed—free to make both trivial and important choices that might not lead to our greater happiness in the long run—but, having given us that freedom, he was even willing to offer as a sacrifice his Beloved Son, who stepped forward to rescue us by absorbing the punishment that justice demands and offering us mercy instead, if we would repent. It's an example to contemplate when our children are troubling us with their pointlessly idiotic insistence on doing things their own way, even if we are certain that we could demonstrate fifty times over that what they have in mind will simply make life more difficult later on. Maybe they need to learn that themselves, or maybe the lesson that is being taught is for *you.* Maybe you just need to learn enough tolerance of their individuality to let them try it their way.

It is also true that allowing for individuality does not apply only to coping with our children. Parenting brings with it the glorious opportunity to learn tolerance of the person who is parenting alongside you. Unfortunately, that's sometimes just as difficult as learning to be tolerant of the kids' eccentricities. Trying to keep your mouth shut when the spouse you love is disciplining the child you love and it seems to you that he or she is going about it in the most peculiar fashion tests the resolve of all of us.

Single parenting has its problems and its challenges. Certainly one of the reasons reproduction is done in pairs is to supply two parents so that one of them can take over when the other one has been pushed to the limit and needs to lie down somewhere quietly and think beautiful thoughts for a while. However, parenting on your own does have one glowing advantage: you can parent according to your own parenting style and you are the only person making the mistakes.

It's different with two.

For one thing, the two of you are coming at this whole experience with slightly different perspectives. This is not usually something either of you think about a lot in advance. Unless one or both of you have had the misfortune of having a miserable childhood and thus have spent a lot of time figuring out what you're going to do differently when you have children of your own, you're most likely to believe vaguely that your families were more or less standard and that standard LDS families are run on the same general principles and are therefore generally similar. This is not true.

Unless you have been childhood sweethearts from back in kindergarten and grew up in and out of each other's houses, it's likely that a lot of your most basic assumptions about how a family works are terra incognita to your spouse. You were children in different families, and the most ordinary daily patterns were individual to each of your families. We don't think about the picky little ways in which families are different until we start living with people who grew up in other families. Are shoes kicked off at the door or worn in the house? Is breakfast a communal meal? Is there a sit-down dinner or a catch-as-catch-can at the kitchen counter? Is the television on seldom, for particular programs only, or a comfortable background for whatever else is going on? Are the bathrooms used by one person at a time, or do you have an open-door policy? How warm is the house kept? Are windows open and doors closed, or the other way around? Is one room kept presentable for visitors at all times, or does family life overflow everywhere? Most of us spend at least part of our early months of marriage being astounded to find out, in the first place, that everybody doesn't do things the way we have grown up to find logical and natural, and in the second place, since they don't, that we have to make some conscious compromises about what is going to happen in our brand-new nuclear family, making decisions about issues we never dreamed existed.

Of course, once you add children to the blend, everything gets more complicated. By that time, you've probably got your dinner arrangements and heat levels and bathroom practices down pat; you may well have almost forgotten they ever caused even a transitory hiccup in your domestic bliss. The arrival of children opens Pandora's box all over again, and with greatly increased intensity.

For one thing, what you do with your children is more important than whether or not you wear shoes on the carpet. What seem like small issues in the abstract (how much back talk parents are prepared to accept, for example) turn into major issues if the father or mother of

46

your children is untroubled by what feels to you like an unacceptable level of impudence and you gradually realize that you really find the smarty-pants stuff intolerable, whether it's aimed at you or not.

Or maybe it's a matter of who does the basic child raising in your family. As parents, we are fond of the notion that all decisions are made by the parents jointly, after amicable discussion. Children, however, can usually identify unerringly which parent normally has the say on the spot and which one lays down the rules long range; sometimes one does both, sometimes not. If when you were growing up it was Dad who maintained order, loyally supported by Mom, it's only reasonable that you assume that the normal, sensible way to arrange family life is with the father in charge. Only maybe you married someone who came from a family where it was Mom who did most of the scut work of laying down the rules, loyally supported by Dad. In that case, the two of you have a lot of talking to do with each other, and even so, there will be times when each of you moves automatically to deal with a disciplinary storm in the pattern that you learned at home and the two of you—not to mention the children—discover you are both sailing in with absolute confidence and at complete cross-purposes. Sometimes those occasions make very funny family stories, but usually not until long, long afterwards.

That's where the tolerance comes in.

Most of us are fortunate enough to love the people we're married to. We also love our children. When the two of you are going at parenting from different angles, it's terribly easy to feel pinned between child and spouse, particularly if the line the child's other parent is taking is more severe than the one you would choose, left to yourself. The fact is that no two people react to aggravation just alike, and just as sometimes you make disciplinary mistakes one way or the other, so will the person you're married to. One of the lessons in tolerance that parenting teaches us is the necessity to be tolerant of each other's mistakes, even when you know it's a mistake at the time.

We may find some comfort in reminding ourselves that few of the errors that well-intentioned parents make are likely to do the children much significant harm anyway. So what if David winds up being grounded for two weeks when you think keeping him in for one Friday night makes enough of a point? If nothing else, the whole experience should point out to David that different people may give different weight to the same misdemeanor. By misbehaving, he made himself liable for punishment, and if he got a judge who handed out a stiffer punishment than he expected, that's his bad luck. If he had been behaving himself, the problem wouldn't have come up. Not a bad lesson, come to think of it.

If we don't give birth to clones, we don't marry them either. It's not only the male-female differences between us that make any given set of mother and father react somewhat differently to their children. Part of it simply comes from our basic personalities shining through. After all, as separate individuals we differ in such unimportant details as what foods we crave or detest (there are those who relish garlic, those who can't stand fish, and even some true eccentrics who don't care for ice cream), and we learn to be fondly tolerant of each other about these things. It is hardly surprising that our individuality is also expressed in such an important business as relating to the children you have in common. We usually have enough sense to work out the major issues in advance—Church activity, for example, and whether or not preparing for college is a given. As always, it's in connection with the little stuff that we discover we're working on inconveniently conflicting assumptions. Is a fixed bedtime written in stone or flexible depending on circumstances? Is enforcing piano/flute/violin/bassoon practice a solemn parental duty, or is compliance to be left up to the child, with the penalty for skipping practice being immediate termination of lessons? To what extent are the children to help around the house, and what relationship do allowances, if any, have to completion of chores? Families work out fine on this kind of stuff no matter what they decide, even if it isn't the way you were brought up and feels kind of strange to you.

One of the complications, of course, is that all of us tend to be encumbered with the defects of our virtues. You fell in love with George because he was so strong in his faith, unabashedly sure of himself, and totally and completely dependable. With George, you could comfortably put your head on his shoulder and know that he would steer your marital ship with poise and firmness. The only trouble, now that you've acquired a child or two, is that George is still certain that his view of any situation is the only conceivable view and the children that have sprung from his loins are as sure of themselves as he is, except that father and child do not always see eye to eye and neither party is inclined to recognize that the other might have a point. This tends to leave you muttering about immovable objects and irresistible forces and wishing you could just go hide in a closet until tomorrow or maybe ten years from now.

Or maybe it was easygoing Megan who won your heart. She bobbed along with engaging optimism and was always inclined to believe the best of anyone. She didn't get upset if things went wrong and could almost always figure out what needed to be done to retrieve any disaster. She was warm and laughing and thought you were wonderful. So Megan the amiable became your wife and the mother of your children, and you have the uneasy feeling the children could be swinging from the rafters and Megan would be chuckling comfortably in the middle of the chaos, pointing out how energetic and creative they are. You cling to your trust in her ability to pull back from the edge of disaster and try not to wonder if her definition of disaster and yours will remain within shouting distance of each other.

This, of course, may well be another reason why the divine plan calls for parents in pairs. That way he can make up for what he sees as her lapses in common sense and she can nobly compensate for what she is convinced are his. Given the fact that these days fathers are getting much more involved in parenting than their fathers ever did, this interplay increasingly goes on on a daily basis. Back in the days when Dad went off to work and Mom ran everything until Dad came home (unless of course Dad headed out immediately again for meetings down at the church, in which case Mom continued running everything at home), the separate spheres kept Mom and Dad out of each other's hair most of the time when it came to parenting. Now that Mom is often out at work, too, and Dad is expected—and expects himself—to take a more active role with the children than simply presiding at the dinner table and supervising activities on Sunday, they find themselves much more tightly interlaced.

Probably what we all need to do is give each other a little space. Tolerance of each other's parenting style often means to step back and let your partner have a crack at it. Moms who are trying to do it all at once, especially those who recognize that the realities of the household budget mean that it all has to go on being done, genuinely need help with the responsibility. If Dad is really going to take on part of the responsibility—as opposed to merely following directions—he's going to want to do it his way.

Two different people, even two different people who love each other, won't handle every single problem exactly the same way, and that's not a bad thing. You can even learn from each other. Maybe you'll see the children respond better to a looser rein from time to time; maybe you suddenly realize that you haven't been taking the time to sit down and listen to what the kids have to say the way your spouse does. Maybe, if you're the one who is more laid back, you find that the children kind of relax in the security of rules they can count on. Two minds working together *can* be more efficient than one.

And what if one of you, following his or her own style, does have a bad day? Maybe you trail in wearily from a day at work to discover that your husband, who got home before you, had his mind on something else and nobody's homework is under way, Darren has been banished to his room for no clear reason, the twins are having a furious argument out in front of the house, and there's Play-Doh in the carpet. So maybe the first step then is to remember the perfectly awful scenes *he's* walked into in his time (or if he hasn't it was purely by grace and fortune, because goodness knows things have fallen apart on your watch from time to time) and decide to start over. Maybe you can even take the whole crowd to McDonald's or wherever for dinner to give you all a respite over burgers and fries. You can tackle homework later, and the Play-Doh tomorrow (it comes out easier when it's dry anyway). Even if you're absolutely sure it was your husband's fault that things got into such a mess, to the extent that "fault" means anything dealing with children, pointing fingers doesn't help. Poor old Darren, however unjustly accused, will gain more from a cheerful parental solidarity that lets bygones be bygones. One of the greatest strengths you can give your child is the knowledge that his parents are a sturdy, indivisible unit, even if they do glare at each other sometimes.

Tolerance doesn't mean simply ignoring our differences. Tolerance means coming to accept them and recognize the different strengths we bring to each other. Maybe your children will turn out to be exactly what you dreamed of and hoped for; more likely what you dreamed of and hoped for will undergo a sea change of sorts, and in the end you'll recognize that what your children are turning into is something richer and better than you could have ever imagined because some of what they uniquely and splendidly are has gone into the blend. Maybe the two of you, husband and wife, will spend years arguing subtly in public and furiously in private over the best methods of child management and never really come to full agreement on either theory or practice, and in the end discover that the children survived you both and your marriage has grown and mellowed from the pushing and pulling into the soft, sturdy pliability of fine leather.

To accept what is familiar and comfortable is easy. To move past acceptance and learn to love the ways our children differ from us (however peculiar we sometimes think they are) is in the end to our benefit, soul-enlarging and rewarding in the way all the hard lessons reward us once we've mastered them.

Maybe—and this would be the most magnificent re-ward—the loving tolerance we've acquired by learning to make allowances for each other can be expanded to the wider world around us. Surely if we can learn to love each other, we can learn to get along with those outside our closest circle. Having struggled to stretch our souls with our children and the one we married, we may even find the flexibility we need to reach out to touch fingertips with the rest of our Heavenly Father's family on this earth, however odd they may seem to us.

They can't be all that much odder than the ones we love have been.

4

Patience

Only Disaster Happens Quickly

Patience is a funny thing. If as a parent you don't start out patient by nature (and obviously not all of us do), parenting draws it out of you. You have to be patient: nothing positive in parenting happens as fast as you'd like it to. Not your children's character development, and not yours, either.

Patience is kind of a pedestrian virtue, made up, I guess, of about equal parts of unselfishness and tolerance. Patience requires you to approach problems by accommodating yourself to someone else and his or her rhythms. This may be something as simple as picking up the spoon the baby drops over the edge of the high chair fourteen times in a row (because the baby is practicing the marvelous new skill of letting something go) or something as complicated as spending whatever time it takes to guide the adolescent into a recognition of his or her

53

own responsibility for actions, teaching that nobody "makes" you do anything, a point that will probably have to be made repeatedly before the concept sinks in. (After all, listening to the talk shows, it would seem that a considerable proportion of the adult population is still whining about what somebody else made them do.) Patience means not stopping when you're ready to stop but hanging in there as long as you need to be there. Patience takes love and compassion and understanding and—well, patience.

Patience isn't a particularly flashy virtue: we don't erect statues to people for their outstanding command of patience. Sometimes it seems that patience is even considered to be a subtle indication of an attitude that's less than vigorous, less than virile and masterful. Is it more glorious to get out and do something or to stand patiently by? It's a choice we face over and over in parenting, and sometimes the hardest test is deciding whether this is the right time *not* to do something. Not giving in to the fight that your fifteen-year-old is trying to pick with you, for example. Is she trying to get at you? You bet. Is she pushing all your buttons? She's doing her best. Would fighting with her get either of you anywhere? Well, for a start, she's fifteen. She's feeling generally aggrieved with life in general, her hormones are probably whipsawing her, and she's stuck in a stage where neither the privileges of adulthood nor the comforts of childhood are really accessible. Would fighting about whether she should clean up her room now (which is your position) or sometime in a vague future (hers) address any of those issues? Not likely. So you stand there and listen to her go on and on and try counting to ten or twenty or maybe a hundred and forty-two and wonder if you're being patient or simply lack disciplinary skills. You know while she's this upset she isn't going to listen to anything you say, no matter how brilliantly phrased it might be. So you go on trying to be patient, hoping somewhere in the back of your mind that eventually the scene will end with her getting started on the room, however sulkily.

There is also the point that the demands for patience don't usually come up when you're braced and ready to be heroic. Take this hassle about the room. Did you plan for anything like this? Well, actually, what you had in mind for this chunk of time was getting dinner started and running a couple of errands that need to be done before five. You just happened to pass the door of her room and mention that you expected that room to be tidied up, and this has been going on ever since. It is now four-thirty, so on top of everything else you are aware of the clock ticking and are reorganizing your plans mentally while trying to keep that muscle in your cheek from twitching with irritation. Does patience get easier with practice? I wonder.

The essence of patience is that you are adapting to conditions you didn't set up, so you're apt to get stuck when you least expect it. You get to practice patience standing there in your underwear trying to get going in the morning. You have to be patient about something else when the pot on the stove is on the point of boiling over and when it will take just one more nail to finish the job, if you could just have an uninterrupted minute to do so. When you have more than one child, you too often need to practice patience with one child at exactly the moment when you were trying to concentrate on another. It doesn't help that nobody generally notices when you're being patient. What gets noticed is when your control slips and you become outstandingly impatient and start demanding that people accommodate themselves to *your* requirements/necessities/schedule. That gets everybody's outraged attention right away.

The continuing need for patience reminds us that there may be speed-reading and speed-writing, but there's no such thing as speed child raising. The whole process goes on at the inexorable pace of a glacier grinding down a slope of rocks (which is pretty close to what it feels like, some days). You can jump up and down, you can bellow with exasperation, but your children will persist in being children, and your abilities to push them into moving along faster on anything—particularly on their rate of physical maturation, which has more to do with everything else than we sometimes realize—are distinctly limited. All that pushing them usually accomplishes is frustration on their part and high blood pressure on yours. You have to learn patience; you've got no choice.

Being a child does take time, and as parents, we have to learn to allow the time for it. I remember taking a walk with an older cousin and her two-year-old when I was a teenager. It turned out to be an exceedingly leisurely walk—the two-year-old was bound and determined to investigate every bush, mailbox, discarded piece of rubbish, and beetle visible on the sidewalk as we passed. After about ten minutes of this, I looked at my cousin, obviously expecting her to get a grip on the situation and get moving, and she said placidly, "I've decided that children are going to enjoy themselves no matter what you do to them and you might as well allow the time for it."

There are lots of ways to allow the time. We keep bumping up against the fact that children are running on their own timetables. They don't always want to listen to us at the times when it is most convenient for us to dispense wisdom. They want to be informed about where babies come from in the middle of a crowd where they've suddenly noticed the difference between the pregnant and non-pregnant female shape. They want to discuss death when you're trying to get to an appointment on time. They want to talk about dating issues at 1:25 in the morning. Children, who are creatures of the present, never seem to see why *now* isn't perfectly appropriate. Having grown past that stage to the adult arts of evasion and procrastination, we have to temper our own impatience and try to take a fresh look at the circumstances.

Why can't we walk just a few steps out of the crowd and explain about babies and where they grow? Is the appointment a life-or-death affair or could you find a few minutes to pull over by the side of the road and talk about the stages of life here and hereafter? If it's the middle of the night, get yourself a glass of ice water to wake yourself up and muffle the yawns and listen to what your teen is trying to say. What better time is there to discuss the emotions of physical attraction than when they are hot and fresh in the memory? After all, chances to speak heart to heart are as scarce as gold. In real life, parental patience is required in a multitude of shapes, in a multitude of places.

Part of the problem of acquiring that patience is that we start out so eagerly. We can hardly wait to get to the fun stuff. With our first babies we are so excited about the reality of this brand-new little person that we want it all to happen right now. We happily gallop through infancy and early childhood, leaping from milestone to milestone. We read the books and anxiously monitor the progress to make sure that Baby is keeping up, right on schedule. First smile, rolling over, sitting up, walking around the edges of the furniture, first independent step, first word—we're ready. No sooner is one accomplishment proudly recorded in the baby book than we are watching impatiently for the next one.

Typically, we're *too* eager. A lot of the stuff blamed on first-child syndrome comes from novice parents simply expecting too much. Heck, we don't know. We're learning, too, and one of the first things we learn is that there are things you can't rush. Take toilet training, for example, which is generally the first battlefield for mother and child where mother can encourage and exhort but the child is the one who has to either go or refrain from going. (We will encounter many other such challenges.) What we all come to learn is that you can't toilet train a child before the child is physically capable of control. It's perfectly true that very young children have reportedly been "trained," but according to the physiologists who make it their business to understand physiological development, what's "trained" is the caretaker, who has to be intently alert and pick up the subtlest clues and spring immediately into action. That is, indeed, one way to do it. The other is to wait until the child has grown into the control, and the waiting is where patience comes in.

With subsequent children, we've learned some of this stuff. For one thing, we're not so worried about keeping up with the prototype baby of the charts and the manuals. We dare to relax. We have discovered that normal children normally learn all the basic normal skills. They just do it in their own sweet time. With experience, you move past your haunted nightmares that your firstborn was still going to be carrying a bottle at thirty, or be married in a diaper. You have learned that by the time children go to school they walk and they talk and which of them was the first to achieve those accomplishments has become irrelevant. They are all weaned and all toilet trained, even if the teacher does want a spare pair of pants for accidents.

Patience even has its rewards. Once we realize that normal developmental successes don't require breathless vigilance, we can comfortably wait for them. There is even much to be said for the advantages of not having yet mastered a skill: a baby who lies adorably on her back is not only satisfactory to coo at, but she *can't go anywhere.* This means she can be left on the floor while you run into the next room (often to check on why the fully mobile children are being so quiet). The baby may follow you with her eyes, but that's about it. You don't yet have to prevent her from splashing in the toilet bowl or stretch netting over the top of her crib to keep her from climbing out or barricade the stairs until she figures out how to turn around and go down backwards. You now know all that's coming, but for the present she simply stays put until you scoop her up, and to add to her charms, she's soft and round and chuckles when you blow bubbles on her tummy. Being patient with exactly where she is and exactly what she is is no problem at all.

Wouldn't it be wonderful if we could feel that way about the children all the time? Wouldn't it be wonderful to just live in the moment? Wouldn't it be wonderful if you could just sit down and wait for Jimmy to tie his own shoelaces with painstaking deliberation and slowness, amused by the concentration on his face and the funny little furrows in his forehead? Wouldn't it be wonderful if you could work on spelling with Steve and simply enjoy the way his hair tufts up on the top of his head, even if he is paying considerably more attention to the dog under the table than to his list on top of it and consequently is spelling the same word wrong for the fourth time? Wouldn't it be wonderful if it didn't matter whether or not Emily gets back with the car when she said she would, and you could spend the twenty-two minutes waiting for her before she eventually gets home calmly admiring the spring bulbs around the tree in front?

The trouble is that none of us have world and time enough. In fact, we're probably not supposed to. If there's anything that living in this world forces us to develop, it's some arrangement of priorities, whether they're always consciously set or not, and it seems hard to believe that that's accidental. Sure, we were sent here to make choices, but one of the reasons we have to make choices is that we haven't been given enough time to do every-thing. We have to make our selection of which things we are going to do based on a day of finite length—exactly twenty-four hours, in fact. Parenting may be a vitally im-portant part of that day, but it's not the only part, and even if some of the parts are uninteresting and routine, they still have to get done. You have to get you to work and Jimmy to school on time (with or without shoelaces being tied by Jimmy himself); you cannot spend the fore-seeable future with Steve and his spelling and the dog because you've got Alice and the outline for her social studies report waiting; and it is essential that you get to the cleaner before it closes, which you won't be able to do if Emily doesn't get that car back right this minute.

For all those reasons we as parents develop patience or ulcers or possibly both. We try to set up rules and make flexible arrangements to minimize the sources of conflict, and sometimes those things work. We recognize that children are by their nature childishly self-absorbed, and one of our obligations is to teach them that as mem-bers of a family and a society they have to adapt them-selves, to some degree, to the needs of others. As the kids get older, we hope that that idea becomes more familiar and accepted. When everything falls apart for whatever reason, as it inevitably will on occasion, we are forced into patience for the simple reason that usually impatience takes even longer.

Patience sustains us through teaching the same things over and over. Sometimes we have to keep repeating ourselves because a particular child has decided that she isn't listening, doesn't want to know, and won't know; much more often it's because we're trying to teach something the child isn't ready for yet. We're working on generosity toward a younger brother, and she still hasn't come to terms with jealousy. It's like being determined you're going to start planting your garden just as soon as the ground thaws, and on the first vaguely warm day you poke the seeds into soggy, wet clumps of earth. The seeds rot and nothing happens when the seed packet says it should, so you stick in some more seeds, and still nothing much happens, and then suddenly when the soil has dried out and the warm days come the little green sprigs finally appear.

It would be wonderful if we had anything as unambiguous as little green sprigs to track the progress of our children. Patience gives us the faith that something's happening even when there isn't much visible sign of it. (After all, they're our kids with our genes, and do we march steadily toward virtue ourselves at an easily tracked, consistent pace?) Some things you need to go over and over again with one particular child. Why? Who knows?

Sometimes it may be something as apparently straightforward as getting your daughter to hang up her coat and book bag when she comes in the door as an alternative to dumping them on the hall floor. This is not a complicated concept. So why, when you've reminded her yet again about it on Monday, do you also have to remind her on Tuesday, Thursday, and Friday? Wednesday was a fluke; she remembered to hang them up on her own, which gave you the wild hope that the system was mastered, hope only to be dashed on Thursday and Friday when everything was dumped, yet again, in the hall. You don't want to start out nagging the second she gets in the door; that's a crummy way to greet her straight back from the day at school. On the other hand, how hard can it be for her to take the minute to hang her things up, particularly when you have explained repeatedly that you are sick to death of the stuff perpetually being on the floor? More relevant, how long is it going to take to get past this basic stuff to something more complicated, like getting whatever homework she's been assigned completed before she turns on TV?

It feels worse when the lesson that needs to be taught over and over again is one that you feel the child should have command of more or less by nature. We're funny about that: there are problems that you can share with your friends and problems that you are less comfortable about admitting to. The difficulty is that both kinds may need exactly the same patience to cope with.

With Kevin's terrible table manners you can simply grit your teeth and endure and remind him over and over again that napkins go in your lap, elbows stay off the table, you generally eat with knives and forks, *not* fingers, and when you're chewing you keep your mouth closed and all sound effects should be as minimal as possible. No big deal, even if it goes on for months, although you might tense up if grandparents are present or if the family goes out to eat anything more elaborate than fast food.

But what if Kevin's table manners are fine, but you have come to the heartsick recognition that you simply cannot necessarily believe what he says? You want to trust him; you know that we have to be able to trust each other, but the facts are fairly clear. I don't suppose it really matters whether we say he tells fibs or tells lies; whichever it is, he's old enough to grasp the distinction between truth and falsity and clearly chooses to say what's convenient, whether it's accurate or not. If it were table manners, you could joke with a good friend about his being a social deviant, but you're not laughing when you find yourself wondering despairingly if he's a moral deviant. Taking months to get his table manners straightened out is irritating, but it's just a matter of hanging in there and doing it; the idea that it may take months to work out a problem like telling the truth terrifies you and intensifies your guilty sense that you must have done something really wrong to have such a serious problem come up at all.

What you need, of course, is exactly the same patience you would bring to the table manners problem. Just as you would keep an eye on how much he was stuffing in his mouth in a single mouthful, so you independently verify every piece of information he gives you that sounds unlikely. When he protests, you explain calmly that when trust has been forfeited, it takes a long time to build it back. You want to believe him, and when you have discovered often enough that you can believe him, you'll be able to go back to believing him in the first place. In the meantime, he needs to know you're checking. Should you discover he's still taking liberties with the truth, you bring each instance you come upon promptly to his attention and administer whatever consequences you have told him are appropriate, and you go on doing that as long as you need to.

When it's table manners, we have no problem assuring Kevin the rest of the time (when we aren't at the table) that he's a great guy and we love him. We need patience raised to the heroic degree to maintain the same even-handedness when the problem is something like being untruthful. The unfortunate fact is that Kevin probably needs the reassurance even more. Making a mess at the table usually is based solely on physical clumsiness and lack of interest in the niceties; the child who tells people what he thinks they want to hear whether it's true or not usually has some problems with what he thinks of himself and lives with the fear that he will be unacceptable if he admits to any failures. Preaching at him won't help unless the preaching is accompanied by a lot of love directed at catching him when he *is* being acceptable and assuring him that he is surrounded by parental devotion regardless of what he does. You may deplore his deeds and go to considerable lengths to foil him, but it's not because you don't love him. You can even try the old saw of explaining to him that if you didn't love him, you wouldn't make such a fuss about what he does, but he probably won't buy that until long years later, when he has grown up to be a pillar of society and is raising his own problematical children. Then he'll know it's true, but his children won't believe it either.

In the meantime you get to live with the guilt and the shame, because by the very nature of these problems with integrity (maybe it's not telling lies; maybe it's taking things that don't belong to him) other people get involved, and you have to deal with them knowing about your son's transgressions. The normal human tendency is to want to dissociate yourself as much as possible; the parental necessity is to stand by his side no matter what you think they're thinking. In the middle of all the guilt and the shame you have to go on patiently loving and teaching, over and over, until the lesson sinks in.

In the bleak moments maybe it helps to remember Jesus' example. He dealt with a lot of others' misdeeds during his ministry, and he didn't seem to think that any of those deeds were so dreadful that his love couldn't cope with them. Remember the woman taken in adultery? Adultery is about as serious a sin as there is, and there she was, guilty beyond doubt—taken in the very act, they said. According to Mosaic law, she should be stoned. Jesus didn't seem to recoil in distaste. Apparently he didn't speak to her or anybody else at first; he just knelt down and wrote on the ground with his finger. I remember once reading the intriguing suggestion that what he wrote was a list of all the sins that her accusers had committed, simply writing them down one after another. I liked that idea. In any case, what he said when he spoke was, "He that is without sin among you, let him first cast a stone at her." One by one, the accusing crowd melted away, and when they had all gone, he asked the woman who accused her, and she answered, "No man, Lord." And Jesus told her, "Neither do I condemn thee; go, and sin no more." (John 8:3–11.)

He didn't tell her she was innocent; he told her to start over, and in doing so he gave us an example to show that where you start out isn't what makes the difference. It's where you get to.

The destination counts. Patience doesn't mean abdicating responsibility and letting our children be whatever they will be. We have to find the patience to stay by the side of our children, teaching and counseling, no matter how long it takes. Sure, we might be tempted at times to throw up our hands and walk away. There's no reason to believe that Satan considers fathers and mothers out-of-bounds for his devious suggestions, and when our children are recalcitrant and ungrateful and a general embarrassment to us, the idea of just pretending it has nothing to do with us can sound quite reasonable. It also happens to be wrong.

We're all here to learn self-control and self-mastery, and some of us learn it one way and some of us learn it another. Only a few of us get away with problems as trivial as table manners. As a matter of fact, if for some wild reason they administered truth serum at any ward outing, you would probably discover that more good brothers and sisters than you can imagine have dealt with problems as serious as any you're dealing with. It's just that they're no more eager to publicize them than you are.

The bottom line, however, is that even if everybody stood up and shared publicly just exactly what's going on at their house, it wouldn't make any difference, really. What other people are coping with or failing to cope with isn't the issue. As parents, we have the obligation to teach our children. We don't get to choose what lessons, and whether anyone is looking at us with raised eyebrows or with the compassion of shared experience is supremely irrelevant. Our assignment is the task at hand.

It would be a lot less taxing to have to teach only the comfortable lessons, but as we discover over and over again, nobody ever said this was going to be easy. We have to teach whatever it is that our particular children have to learn, and maybe what we learn along with them is the invaluable lesson that if you're doing what you know you should be doing—which is teaching your child with steadfastness and love—then what anybody else, apart from the Lord, thinks about it doesn't matter. At some point in every parent's life we have to decide whether we're raising our children to satisfy the neighbors (whether that means the people down the block or the ones down at the ward) or to fulfill the stewardship we have been given, and there's only one good answer.

Even so, the chances are excellent that we won't get it right every single time. When we're thinking about patience and parenting, we have to remember to apply a liberal dose of that patience to ourselves. Parenting is complicated and challenging enough that we're going to take a lot of stabs at it before we figure it out, and we might just as well be prepared for that.

For one thing, it's like writing on water. Nothing stays put. You finally worked out the precise blend of patience and affection necessary to persuade Annemarie to unfasten herself from your left leg in order to leave her in the nursery on Sunday, but then it feels like you blinked once and the problem underwent a metamorphosis. Now instead of persuading her not to cling, you have to find a way to teach her that she must not dart away into the thick of the shopping mall crowd the minute you pause to look at a window display or rearrange the bags you're carrying. The patience and firmness you developed while helping her learn to separate from you might need to be applied in some different ways when you're hurling yourself after her disappearing back, but you still need them to persuade your two-year-old bent on adventure that when you say, "Stay here with me," that's exactly what you mean.

Because the children are growing up, they are in a constant state of change. What they need from you changes, too, sometimes from one day to the next, and you are not alone if you discover that your patience holds out better at some of the stages than at others. We are all individuals, and we express our individuality in our child-raising styles as much as in anything else. I know a man who is absolutely wonderful dealing with babies. He loves them; they adore him, and his patience with them is apparently limitless. As his own children grew into the leggy school-age stage, he found them somewhat harder to get along with. He didn't have a lot of time for the kind of smart-alecky behavior that third- and fourth-graders are so good at. He was still a good father, because he loves his kids even when they exasperate him and takes his responsibilities seriously, but it took more out of him. The interesting part is that when his children turned the corner into adolescence, they blossomed once again into a stage he found inherently attractive. All the things that drive the rest of us nuts about kids that age—their stubbornness, their prickly insistence on their own right to make decisions, their carefully masked uncertainties— are comprehensible and endearing to him. Restless teenagers can talk to him, and while they may not necessarily immediately follow his counsel (he does not, after all, walk on water), they at least listen to it, and it clearly makes more impact than they might be prepared to admit at the time. I suppose one of his strongest assets is exactly that natural patience that the rest of us struggle to imitate: the kids, sensing that he is going to stay right there for them, can lean back and rest on the unspoken reassurance that they're all right and things are going to work out fine. Even when he cracks down on them (and he does), the kids figure he's fundamentally on their side—I guess because they know he genuinely enjoys them.

It's a gift, but we all have gifts. Some of us enjoy the school-age stage most and get a kick out of pretend Halloween spookiness and the irrepressible energy of Cub pack meetings; some of us particularly treasure our babies, and long after they have left diapers and cribs and first pairs of shoes far behind, we find ourselves looking at the snapshots of the way they were and remembering their soft roundness in our hands and what the total peace of sitting in a rocking chair with a sleeping baby felt like. It's not surprising that you find your patience is longer during the periods you like best; one of the reasons you like them and find that patience comes naturally is undoubtedly that you're good at that particular stage. Fortunately, being better at one stage doesn't mean you can't get a handle on the others. You'll get through them just fine, even if they take more conscious effort. All you need is a little more patience with yourself and some trust in the Lord.

After all, parenting is one of the Lord's best ways to coax us into maturity. As we're struggling to increase our patience with our children, we are stretching muscles that we need to develop for ourselves. Sometimes we stretch muscles by dealing with major difficulties; much more often we're forced into developing our capacity for patience and love by being presented with a succession of trivial annoyances to deal with. Sometimes, when you're beset by one exasperation after another, it's tempting to believe that it would almost be easier to have just one major crisis of such sufficient dimension that nobody would expect you to continue coping with everything else at the same time; this is usually the kind of thing you think only when you don't have a major crisis going to remind you how soul shattering they can be. In any case, we usually don't get to pick what kind of trials we are expected to endure: as an academic exercise it might be interesting to argue whether it would be more challenging to be a pioneer crossing the plains or a Primary president in a ward where the teachers keep calling in sick at the last minute and the Blazers won't stop shoving each other and making rude remarks during sharing time, but since the pioneers got there a long time ago, in practical terms it's not really a choice open to us. We cope with what we're given, which is probably a bunch of kids whom we love devotedly and who test our patience on a regular basis.

Patience can mean a lot of things. Patience can mean keeping your hands off, letting children have a crack at working things out for themselves. Sometimes it's standing to one side while she struggles with putting on a sweater or a pair of shoes; sometimes it's refusing to run interference and letting him serve the detention he earned by cutting up in class, even if it means that a whole complicated cat's cradle of after-school activities has to be rearranged. Of course patience can equally well mean getting in there up to your elbows. Maybe it's something as simple as catching the ball over and over and still over again, because she wants so badly to make the team and her brother and sisters have balked at practicing anymore with her. Maybe it's as hard on your ego as continuing to offer the best counsel you can muster again and again, even though the son you're counseling is doing his utmost to make it obvious that he doesn't want to hear anything you're saying and keeps telling you he wishes you would go away instead of continuing to remind him of what he won't admit he knows he should be doing.

Whether it's hands-on or hands-off, it's practically guaranteed that you won't see the results of what you've been doing as soon as you wish you would. Children are generally ill-adapted to providing instant positive feedback. We get about eighteen years to work with for each child, and some of what we want most to teach them (the solidity of testimony to sustain them; a vigorous sense of their own worth; a comfortable confidence in relating to the rest of the Lord's children) takes every bit that long, and if you're a typical parent, along the way you'll be getting some feedback that will make you wonder if you're making any headway at all. The more important the issue, the longer it takes to reap the harvest we hope we've been planting. Sometimes what we need most of all is faith—faith in what we're trying to teach to them, faith in our own ability to do it, and faith that our Heavenly Father is parenting right alongside us. After all, these vulnerable, endearing, infuriating children are his children, too.

We all want to be the perfect parents for each of the children. It would be wonderful to be perfect people. It's much harder to be uncertain about what you're doing or to wonder if you're getting it wrong. Wouldn't it be wonderful to be right from the very beginning! Instead, being fallible human beings and not perfect automatons, it takes us a while, and sometimes we have to make mistakes to learn from them. Sometimes, particularly when you have the feeling that you're being asked for more patience than you can imagine yourself being capable of, you just have to rely on the Lord. His patience is infinite; maybe with his help you can hang out a little longer on the last shreds of patience you thought you possessed, finding just that little bit more with the kids, more with your spouse (who probably has just about had it, too), and most of all, more patience with yourself, with your own false starts and your own misdirected efforts. Maybe it will even turn out like the loaves and fishes and you'll manage to go further and with a lighter heart than you had imagined possible.

We all make mistakes. We start out not knowing beans about the business (except for maybe some theories, most of which will probably turn out to be impractical). Parenting is too all-consuming to be managed unerringly. Of course you'll make mistakes. Your parents did: even those of us who have the happiest memories of our own childhood can usually remember a couple of things that could well have been done differently. Some of us can produce a very long list indeed. Mainly we mean well in our turn, but we keep being hounded by inconsistency and tripped up by irritation and our own imperfections—never mind anybody else's.

Will we ever be as patient as we need to be? I do hope so, but my experience doesn't lead me to be all that optimistic. I can get up in the morning determined to be as patient as Job, and by ten o'clock I've lost it a couple of times, once because the child I was trying to urge along so gently and sweetly dawdled sufficiently to miss the bus and had to be driven, and once because a particularly inaccessible light bulb blew and when I was engaged in the replacement effort, the children boiled up around me with one of their senseless arguments and I managed to break off the base in the socket. (Since I couldn't honestly say it was anybody else's fault, I had to gripe at myself.) I'm not there yet, but I still do have the children here at home to serve as motivation to hone my skills. Maybe the right question to ask is if I am getting any better than I have been.

For some of us patience comes easier than for others. Whether it does or not, we are pushed and chivvied into behaving like more patient people, and maybe in the end, the appearance comes to be the reality. Of course, by that time we won't be grappling with the parenting problems. We'll be watching our impatient children struggle and trying to keep our amusement from showing too visibly while we play with the grandchildren. We've been through the mill; it's their turn to ponder over when to speak up and when to keep silent.

The wheel turns, and I expect we'll be hurried on to new lessons. What does the Lord intend me to do with all this uncomplaining patience I'm acquiring? I can't imagine, but I'm sure down the echoing halls of eternity I will find out.

When I need to know, I will. All I need now is the patience to wait.

5

Self-Control

The Management
of Tempers

We don't need major confrontations to step onto the battlefield of self-control. Plain ordinary parenting offers more than sufficient provocation for us to fly off the handle. Everyday life is full of opportunity; it doesn't have to be anything that's a big deal. It's true that the precise details of what happens at my house may not be exactly what happens at yours—and maybe stuff that drives me crazy strikes you funny (or vice versa)—but we are all familiar with that feeling that is illustrated in the cartoons by a character turning bright red and puffing steam out of his ears. It may be triggered inadvertently, maybe by Andy wandering thoughtlessly off for the fiftieth time (at least), leaving the back gate wide open so that the dog bounds out contrary to all the local leash laws, charging through flower beds, treeing the cat two doors down, and alienating the neighbors, who clearly are coming to the conclusion that your dog or your son or both are in dire need of some meaningful discipline. It may be triggered very deliberately, maybe by Jennifer tossing her head defiantly and staring you straight in the eye as she announces she isn't going to do whatever it is, and you can't make her. However it happens, we're all familiar with the feeling.

At such moments, the concept that you are unlikely to be able to control much of anything if you can't control yourself is not precisely what you want to hear, but it's still true.

As a society, we're oddly ambivalent about self-control. We talk about the necessity of teaching children self-control, probably most often in the context of resisting the modern-day temptations of drugs and easy violence. On the other hand, there seems to be a psychological subtext that leans toward the notion that natural is best and that thwarting natural impulses is somehow unhealthy. That psychological subtext almost certainly originated back in the eighteenth century with the French philosopher Jean-Jacques Rousseau. Rousseau was an odd bird, to say the least: in the course of an exceedingly irregular lifestyle he and his mistress, according to his own account, had five children, each of which they took to the foundling hospital and abandoned immediately after birth. (This bit of autobiography has been challenged by modern scholars as possibly untruthful, which would presumably mean Rousseau was less irresponsible than we thought but even more eccentric to circulate such a story in the first place.) Such personal deviations aside, Rousseau's thinking was enormously influential in his time and afterwards. He came up with the idea that by nature man is good in a simple way. He is self-sufficient, compassionate to others when they do not threaten him, and incapable of pride, hatred, falsehood, and vice, but has only limited intellectual capacities. The paradox is that society, precisely because it develops man's faculties, corrupts him, and all evil is thus unleashed.

In many ways what Rousseau proposed was an attractive idea to his fellow intellectuals in the decades just before the French Revolution, when the magnificence and corruption of the monarchy was managing to produce the greatest misery for the greatest number of the people. The idea that somehow if all government did not exist man would live in peace and harmony was a seductive one. It has continued to seduce thinkers ever since. Look at the innocence of children, they claim. Look at their sweetness, their purity. It must be society that changes them into the suspicious, selfish, grasping adults who populate our world. If you just left them alone . . .

With the perspective of the gospel, we come at the problem from the other side. In his address to his people King Benjamin made it clear that it is true that children are submissive, meek, humble, patient, and full of love, but that is because they submit to their fathers, and as adults all those virtues are possible to us only if we submit to the Lord in the same way, yielding to "the enticings of the Holy Spirit." "Natural man," said King Benjamin, "is an enemy to God." (Mosiah 3:19.) Rousseau, in other words, was as muddleheaded in his philosophy as in his life, and wrong about both. To base our lives on the natural-is-best philosophy, shunning the dictates of society in the belief that they corrupt innocence and produce pride, hatred, falsehood, and vice, misses the mark; it is only by following the rule of God's law—another way of saying self-control—that we can preserve innocence and prevent those evils from overwhelming us all.

It would certainly seem from watching what is going on around us that King Benjamin's predictions were more accurate than Rousseau's. When society crumbles—as it too often does these days in the areas where poverty and despair and the easy availability of drugs and our universal preoccupation with sexual pleasure have decimated family structure—children do not emerge as noble savages, untutored but good, self-sufficient, and compassionate. They turn out to be predatory beasts, the stronger stalking the weaker. When there is no one willing or able to teach self-control, what happens is anarchy, and anarchy is careless, dysfunctional, and casually cruel.

If we don't teach anything else, we must teach self-control. If we don't manage to master anything else, we must master ourselves.

That's part of the difficulty. What happens is that we have to work on both parts of the problem at once. At exactly the same time that you are teaching one son that he must control the impulse to trip his brother (no matter how funny he looks as he crashes to the grass), you have to haul in the reins on yourself when you discover you're on the point of losing it entirely because he does it one more time anyway.

Is it possible to parent without coming to understand the roots of child abuse? I remember one afternoon when my two youngest children were toddlers. I was probably tired to start out with (I was usually tired at that stage), but at the point that memory kicks in, I discovered the two of them were happily emptying their chest of drawers by dumping the contents down the stairs. Company was due to arrive, as it always is at times like that. When I came up the stairs, of necessity stepping on clothes that up until then had been clean and folded, scolding as I came, the two of them stood together at the top of the stairs and laughed at me.

That was when I skidded off into fury. I put them both in the top bunk of their sisters' bed. I didn't quite throw them there, but it came close. I put them there because I knew I was so angry that if I got my hands on them I might not be responsible. Up in the top bunk they were out of my range while I picked up the mess and retrieved such shreds of self-control as I still possessed.

By that time I had been a mother long enough that the sheer surge of wrath didn't shock me as it might have in the early days. (On the other hand, I don't remember ever being angrier than I was that afternoon.) When we start out with an inoffensive vulnerable baby, few of us anticipate that one of the passions of parenthood is inevitably anger—plain raw anger, one of those basic elemental impulses that we are here to learn to curb. It was depressing, of course, to realize (later that day when I was mulling over the whole experience) that although I'd been around the track for quite a while at that point and presumably learned something in the process, I was still perfectly capable of flying into a rage when sufficiently provoked. I had had many opportunities to deal with the explosive tempers of my children, trying to help them work on the elements of self-control. What was most discouraging was the dreary recognition that I was still struggling with the lessons I was trying to teach them. (It is even more depressing to have to report that I still am.)

It's not that punishing those two toddlers would have been wrong; what would be wrong was that I would have been so angry while I did it. Although I have long been amused by Erma Bombeck's twist on the old saw "Never strike a child in anger"—"Wait until a happier time," she proposed blandly—the fact is that punishing when you are angry is like waving a loaded, cocked gun around. Like the gun, you are only marginally under control, and narrow margins are no basis for responsible decision-making, which is exactly why parental self-control is such an imperative.

That self-control has to come from within. There is no way we can pretend to have it, because life will find us out. If you don't have self-control, you're vulnerable to every whirl and wisp of emotion. You don't decide what happens in your life; that's decided by whatever happens to you.

Self-control isn't just about temper, of course. Self-control is about keeping command of yourself in general. It takes self-control to resist the seduction of passing impulse. It's self-control, for example, that keeps us from putting ourselves in positions where we might be compromised. It would be wonderful if the only person in the world whom you found attractive was your spouse, but that's not usually the way it is. Self-control means taking for granted that you will be attracted from time to time in passing, and that when you are, you smile politely and make absolutely sure that you never find yourself in a situation where it would be easy to give way to it. Being attracted is one thing and can be absolutely innocent; acting on attraction is a different business entirely. It's Satan's idea—enthusiastically adopted by too much of the world—that the simple fact of attraction is justification for following through on it. Self-control requires recognition that anything we choose to do *is* a choice: free will comes into it. We are the children of our Heavenly Father, blessed with accountability, not creatures governed by our glands.

Self-control means other things, too. Self-control is involved in such simple decisions as whether to get down to a job you are not particularly eager to do or to fritter away your time on something you'd feel sheepish about admitting you were up to. This is not to say that you should never be discovered watching something dumb on TV (after all, if you're home with young children, you have to do something while you're folding the endless laundry), but the point is that such a choice ought to be a conscious decision rather than an alternative to getting the bills in order or cleaning the fridge or some other distinctly unthrilling occupation that still needs to be done. Obviously we all have days of turning on the TV or talking on the phone or wasting time in some marginally more creative fashion, and nobody has died of that yet. Nonetheless, time wasting *is* an issue of self-control. Rather a similar situation, when you think about it, to discovering to your irritation that instead of straightening up the family room as asked, your offspring is standing there with dust mop in hand, gawking vaguely into middle distance, or has picked up the Nintendo and, mouth half-open in concentration, is apparently mesmerized by the electronic noises while the mess you wanted cleaned up lies in undisturbed peace: one more demonstration that we're still trying to teach what we're simultaneously trying to learn ourselves.

But the impulsive behavior that gives us as parents the most trouble is probably anger, because it surges up out of nowhere and much of the time it is indeed justified (which broadly means that the children are certifiably capable of being absolutely, flat-out infuriating). Still, if we don't get on top of that, everything else not only can but will go spiraling out of control.

What makes parental anger so critical is the impact of parental power. We tend to discount how much power we have over our children; for one thing, we know our own shortcomings and ordinariness, and it seems incredible that we should cast a particularly long shadow to the people who see us at our most unimpressive—rubbing our noses, yawning and scratching absentmindedly in our pajamas, or maybe peering hopefully into the refrigerator. For a fairer evaluation of the impact of parent upon child, we need to remember back to the influence our own parents have had on us and how heavily their opinions weighed on us then and probably still weigh. Remember the glowing comfort of their approval? Remember the hesitation we felt at the prospect of flying in the face of their disapproval? For some of us, any defiance was something that was never contemplated; for others, it was merely a passing phase of mild rebellion. For still others, our parents' convictions had to be discarded for us to move into the pattern of what we recognize as truth. However it happened, it didn't happen casually. What they thought mattered to us.

The same is true of us and our children. What we say to them matters to them. For one thing, we are the ones who first explain the world to them, and at the beginning we are the fount of all knowledge, as far as they're concerned. They bring their triumphs and disappointments to us first, utterly confident that we have the power to make everything right. And isn't it a good feeling, when the children and the problems are still small, to be able to straighten it all out? Maybe it's something as simple as getting the tricycle and the jump rope, which for some strange reason have become totally tangled together, extricated and separate once more. Your child, who probably created the problem in the first place by trying to tie up the tricycle like a horse, comes running to you, confident that you'll be able to straighten it out, and when you do, takes it gloriously and happily for granted, and you saunter back to the house feeling extremely pleased with yourself. If only everything would stay so simple and we could stay so wise!

We have the privilege of being the ones to tell our children about their Heavenly Father, about the love that will surround them all their lives if they'll just reach out to it, and with the innocence of children, they couple the messenger with the message, and for the rest of their lives, the foundation of their gospel knowledge will carry the faint echo of our voices. We are the first ones to explain to them the principles of righteous living that do in fact make ordinary life easier and more rewarding—basic principles like honesty and kindness to others and doing your best—and so we are the first ones to share with them their delight in discovering that those principles work. All of those things make us very powerful in their eyes.

We can see it easily when they're very little. They think we're wonderful and they are sure we know everything. Whenever anything makes them uncertain, they're inclined to hide behind us, and even as they get bigger, they want to climb into our laps as the safest stronghold from which to watch a suspenseful video or more boisterous roughhousing than usual among older siblings. When they're sick or injured, they turn first to Mom and Dad, and that goes on long after they have begun to grow dubious about whether we really do know everything about anything. (It has always seemed to me that kindergarten really began the slippery slide out of the Garden of Eden at our house. One by one my kindergartners came home convinced that Mrs. Kingston knew stuff that Mom didn't have a clue about.)

But there's another part to our power that we don't always consciously recognize. Our children take their definition of what they believe themselves to be from what they think we believe them to be. If we tell our children they are good about remembering to put away their mittens and boots or very smart to have figured out how to work the microwave, they will believe us. If we tell them they are dumb to keep asking the same question over and over or clumsy because they knocked over the lamp in the living room, they will believe that, too. It doesn't matter that somebody else (maybe the kid next door, maybe a brother or sister) could criticize exactly the same way with no visible repercussions whatsoever. Those are just kids; we're the ones (they believe) who know.

That doesn't mean that you are expected to wander around all the time with a sweet smile on your face and tell your children only positive things about themselves. Children certainly start out innocent and pure, but they don't get to stay that way any more than we did. They grow into the same battles with natural man that we know so well from our own experience, and a lot of times the battlefield is the family turf. Our children can be loving and dear and engaging, and they can also be defiant, deliberately unkind, and spiteful. Our problem is to deal with their inevitable misbehavior without letting our tempers get the best of both of us.

It happens. It happens very easily. Children can drive you batty. Wonderful as a child is much of the time, any child worth raising can test the patience of Job. Children have temper tantrums at the worst possible times and for no good reason that you can figure out. Children can be deliberately disobedient. Children can be careless and impudent, and almost all of them will write on the walls at one time or another, most generally just after you've wallpapered or painted. It can feel as if your child is determined to drive you into a corner, just testing to see exactly how much you will absorb before exploding.

As they get older, they get better at it. Particularly as they get into their adolescent years, our children turn into pompous know-it-alls. They seem inclined to believe that anyone of our generation grew up in some time and place so removed from any reality of the present that we can't possibly know what they're talking about. Quite apart from the fact that I am not a survivor from antiquity, and would rather not be treated like one, I bristle, quite frankly, at the assumption that I'm not very bright, either. The really unfair part (my kids are big on things not being fair) is that when I do get goaded just too far and speak more swiftly and less kindly than I mean to, these irritating sophisticates turn out to be just as vulnerable as they've been all along, and I wind up having to repent for my burst of temper and figure out what I can do in the way of damage control. ("No, I didn't say you were a dork, I said that was a dorky thing to say. *You* are not a dork." Slight pause. "What *is* a dork, anyway?")

In the middle of all our soul-searching about the power we have, it's important to remember the power that we don't. Although we unquestionably have considerable influence over our children, we don't control them and never can. The only person I can control is me. My children, and yours, and everybody else's arrived here as free and separate individuals, possessed of their own thoughts and their own free agency. Whereas it is certainly true that while they are still children I don't necessarily allow them to make their own decisions about everything (whether or not to go to church and whether or not to burn the house down are two biggies that leap immediately to mind), what I have to remember is that they are steadily growing towards their own accountability, and every year there are choices that they are ready to make that they were not ready for the year before. It's my job to help them get ready to make those choices, and then stand back and let them do it.

Put that way, it all sounds as if it should be so easy. It isn't.

Our power over them grows out of the circumstance that we are bigger and more experienced and wiser, we hope. Their power over us is based in the very simple reality that we love them so dearly. I wonder if any of us expect to love our children as much as we do? I know I didn't. I expected to love them, of course, but I didn't expect love to be such an overwhelming experience. I didn't expect my love would make me care so much, and that caring so much would make me so vulnerable. When the kids next door had a party that got out of control and I wound up with soft drink and beer cans on my lawn and the sprinkler bent out of shape, I was very cross. But I hadn't invested my hopes and my dreams and my love in the kids next door. If *my* children did any such thing, I would be livid, and part of my fury would be fueled by my disappointment in them and my guilty worry that somehow I had fallen down on the job of parenting for them to show such a disregard for responsibility.

Maybe that's part of the reason the Lord uses parenting as a tool to refine us. I suppose it is possible to slouch through producing a child and maybe even living with one and remain emotionally distant. After all, there are all those reports of the people who do, although I suspect most of them are anesthetized by drugs of one sort or another or maybe general hopelessness, and their detachment is simply another symptom. But for most of us, having a child brings us nose-to-nose with reality, and reality involves the whole range of human emotions. We can't hide behind an assumed facade of what's proper or appropriate. The intensity of our involvement burns away everything but honesty. Being a parent forces us right out into the arena, to face and cope with our own weaknesses.

Anger has been around for a long time. The book of Genesis talks about anger, and there's quite a lot about it in the section of Proverbs that focuses on the right ways and wrong ways of living. The conclusion, given a couple of times, is that if you're quick to anger you probably aren't thinking clearly and are liable to act foolishly, which most of us parents can verify from our own experience. Note that it's being quick to anger that's identified as the problem. Righteous anger, the kind that Jesus presumably felt when he drove the merchants and the money changers out of the temple in Jerusalem with a scourge of cords he had made himself, is another matter altogether.

Why is the loss of self-control we call losing our temper so well-nigh universal? Well, for one reason, it feels good.

There's a reason an explosion of anger is so often pictured as being similar to a teakettle's coming to a boil with a fine, high plume of steam. That's exactly what it feels like. You start out getting cross and get crosser and crosser, feeling your frustration and fury build up higher and higher while you hang onto your control and try to think reasonably, try to hold back the words that are just bubbling to get out. Then the final straw is added to the pile (whatever it might be), and there at last is the glorious release of just letting fly in any available direction.

That feels good. The problem is coping with the aftermath. Nobody ever said that following the impulses of natural man doesn't feel good at the time; those transitory, here-and-now satisfactions are what make a lot of temptations tempting. A major difference between behaving responsibly and righteously and irresponsibly and selfishly is what happens afterwards. All acts have consequences; when you lose your temper, you have to cope with the responses of the people around you.

In the movies and on television when people lose their tempers, it's frequently dramatized by china and other breakables being hurled around; in real life, I suspect we less often break china than we beat out our temper in words aimed against whoever happens to be closest to the line of fire. When china breaks, somebody has to sweep it up. When a relationship is damaged by saying too much, somebody has to mend that, too.

A lot of maxims have to do with speaking in haste and repenting at leisure, probably because it's a close to universal human experience. It's something that happens, but like floods, fires, and earthquakes, that doesn't mean it's a good thing. Remember the old childhood rhyme?

> Sticks and stones can break my bones
> But words can never hurt me.

That's playground bravado. Words do hurt. We have all been hurt by words, and we have all hurt others at one time or another. All of us have thought thoughts that are less than kind, had cruel thoughts that would cut and slash if you were to say exactly what is drifting across your mind. We get irritated, we feel aggrieved, we feel way too much is being expected of us, and we mutter silently to ourselves, taking careful note of all the inadequacies and stupidities of whoever is (or seems to be) creating our problems. As long as self-control keeps it an internal debate, nobody is much harmed by it, except maybe you if you hug your grievances to yourself and keep counting them over and over. Hopefully, most of the time we gradually simmer down and try to reach a state of sufficient calm so that we can figure out a constructive way to deal with whatever the problem might be.

The danger with abandoning self-control and letting the steam valve blow is that something that you might have thought for only a second or two (and in any ordinary sense don't really mean) suddenly escapes and is spoken. I remember being told once that as long as words are on your tongue, you own them. If you let go in anger, you're going to say something you're going to regret later, and then the words won't belong only to you. They belong as well to the person who heard them.

That's when the damage is done. No matter how much you say, "I didn't mean it," the words are out there and gone, part of the memory of somebody else. It happens to all of us, at one time or another, to a greater or lesser degree, and all of us have known moments of wishing desperately that errant words could be magically recalled—a good point to remember, in fact, when we are the one stabbed through by somebody else's impetuous outburst. Because we are most likely to let our guard down in the comfort of home, it is unfortunately true that the people most likely to bear the brunt of our temper are the ones we love the best—our families.

Having spoken too swiftly and unwisely to a husband or wife is bad enough, but it happens, and the chances are good that unless you married a perfected saint, he or she had a word or two to say back, and the two of you can forgive one another. The problem with speaking spitefully to your children is exactly that question of the power your opinion carries. The balance isn't even, or anywhere near even, and it's knowing that that forces us into a level of self-control that we never would have thought possible in the days before we had our children. We have to learn to catch the words before they are spoken, and most of the time we amaze ourselves by managing to do it.

There are, after all, other ways of dealing with that surge of emotion, other things to do than shout or snipe at the children. There are the old traditional ways: Cleaning house, *hard.* Beating rugs. Kneading bread (the machine shouldn't get all the emotional therapy). The story that has gone down through the generations in our family is that my great-grandmother said it was always worthwhile to get my grandmother cross before there was a major job to be done: angry, she accomplished twice as much. So wash windows, polish silver, all the dumb things you've been avoiding doing. Do them with all your might and not only will you defuse yourself but you'll feel noble at the same time. Try walking around the block vigorously—three or four times if necessary. Try power walking (the arm-swinging method that humorist Dave Barry describes as walking like a dork); if your adolescent children see you and are mortified—they most likely being what set you off—so much the better. If the children are little and right there with you (which is so often the problem; the children *are* there, and you have to be, too), you can try closing yourself in the bathroom and arguing vigorously with your reflection in the mirror. Your sense of humor might even take over and save you from yourself. If the children are pounding on the bathroom door, at least you know where they are.

Sometimes we find it easier to talk about our lives as if we lived in a greeting-card world where everybody is gentle and happy and the sun perpetually shines decoratively. That would be nice, but that doesn't happen to be the world we live in. There may be some blessed exceptions, but most of us walk the edge of the abyss and need faith and determination to keep doing the things we know we ought to do and guard ourselves from being over-whelmed by the temptations that will tumble us over and down.

Being a parent forces us to confront what we most es-sentially are. Parenting is a 24-hour-a-day job, 365 days a year—except for leap year, when we get to spend 366 days at it. Not many of us would be really capable of maintaining a facade for all that time, and if we did, the facade would develop a reality of its own. Parenting isn't a business of fussing with the icing on the cake; parent-ing is the cake itself. With our children we are forced into fundamental honesty, because unless we keep a house-hold staff to look after them day after day, year after year, the children will know us for exactly who we are. They may look to us for a definition of what they can be, but we can see what we ourselves are looking back at us from the reflection in their eyes.

I'll see something different there than you will. We all have our own little ways, our own strengths and our own foibles. I can do perfectly idiotic things that would never occur to you; some of the consummately dumb things you do seem as incredible to me as they do to you, once you've gotten back to thinking straight. Both of us can work on our weaknesses and struggle with our faith and develop our testimonies and perfect ourselves, and when we wind up, as we hope we will, in the celestial kingdom, we'll still be different, because you are what you are and I am what I am.

Some people (generally those who can't understand what we see in the gospel) believe that obedience to rules turns people into interchangeable units by ironing out all their individuality. You need to be free, they say, beating their chests with the expansive enthusiasm of true eman-cipation. You have to follow your own star, be your own self-defined self.

What they don't understand, probably because they're too busy beating their chests to listen, is that it is only by obedience that you free yourself to be what you most truly are. The Lord's commandments don't cramp us in; by freeing us from the consequences of error, they can give the eternal spirits within us a chance to unfold and develop the potential that we've brought with us from the eternities before we came here. And if only everybody obeyed the Lord's laws, all of us would be liberated to explore the possibilities of this world without being hedged in by fear and the need for taking sensible precautions and for watching our backs. Can you imagine how wonderful it would be to be able to walk across any city, even across a park, on a late summer evening under the harvest moon and know you would be safe and unharassed? Imagine being free to feel the cool night breeze and watch the pattern of the moonlight through the trees. So it would be—will be during the Millennium—if all of us loved each other enough to leave one another in peace, respecting free agency, and keeping a firm grip on our own self-control. Those are the foundation blocks of the gospel, and they don't fence us in. It's the lack of them that's confining.

For most of us, parenting is the laboratory in which we are given the cram course in self-control, for starters. We won't all go at it the same way, and we won't all have the same battles to fight (although we'll all probably go a round or two mastering our tempers). After all, we arrive with different temperaments. Even for such a universal problem as coping with anger, we'll go at it from different directions. There are the explosive sorts who have to learn to keep the kettle on simmer and maybe raise your voice from time to time but keep track of what you're saying and why. There are the ones whose anger is cold and unforgiving, and you have to learn to mellow out a little and recognize that perfection is still a step or two down the way not only for you but also for the people around you, and they're going to make mistakes and do dumb things and you can't go on making lists of those things and chewing over the fact of your outrage. There is also that business about forgiving seventy times seven, which my calculator works out as 490 times per offense, and if you're of a record-keeping bent, that should keep you fully occupied.

Self-control really means learning to carry the responsibility for ourselves on our own shoulders. It does sometimes seem unfair that we're having to teach our children the elementary stages of that when we're not anywhere near home free ourselves, but in the course of being parents, we find that happens a lot of the time. Maybe it's because if the Lord waited for us to grow up completely, we'd be ninety years old before we were ready—and without the cold-bath shock treatment of being responsible for endearing, exasperating children, some of us might never make it. Besides, the lesson of self-control is so important that we have to get going with it, whether we feel particularly qualified or not.

Most of the time, answers we work out ourselves are significantly more meaningful than answers that are simply given to us. Consider the average general conference: if we could all absorb all the wisdom offered and rearrange our lifestyles to live in perfect accordance with what we've learned, what a congregation of saints we would have in very short order! In fact, many of us gain the most from the conference talks that reaffirm lessons we've learned ourselves the hard way, so that we recognize the truth and can use the suggestions to help us deal with the lingering remains of whatever problem it might be.

Self-control is like that. Nobody can tell you how to master it; we can only remind one another that it must be mastered. Each of us has to learn to manage our own stubbornness and our own willful tendency to do what we want to do with little or no consideration given to the worthiness of the action, and all of us will lose some of the battles on the way, we pray, to winning the war.

Our children serve as the refining fire. They can be relied upon to back you into corners and to enrage you when you're not prepared to be adult and sensible about it. They go on needing your strength and your forbearance when you have a feverish cold and feel like biting anyone who comes within range, and they need you to be as reasonable and rational when you're coping with a curfew violation in the middle of the night as you might have been first thing in the morning when you were fresh and alert after a good night's sleep, which you're clearly not going to get tonight at the rate things are going.

The challenge of parenthood, since it is a full-time occupation in the most literal sense, is that it forces us into self-control on an equally full-time basis. We learn that we can be free of our passing impulses, free to be the kind of parents our children deserve.

And the real magnificence is this: our children, whether they're trying to or not, can't help but learn from our successes. Every time we manage to listen to what they're saying (howsoever infuriating) and then count to ten or otherwise marshal our resources before coming up with a calm and reasoned response, we are teaching them that anger does not have to be answered with anger. Every time we stop ourselves from wading in, yelling and spanking, we teach them that it is possible to govern yourself. The results may not be immediate; that's another thing we're learning to live with. Nevertheless, you've managed to give them a head start on their own battles, the ones now and the ones to come.

We're all going to have those battles with ourselves, but that doesn't matter. That's exactly what we came to this earth to do, and as we learn over and over, it's not where you start out that makes the difference.

It's where you finish.

6

Humility

Learning by Misadventure

If achieving humility meant only coming nose-to-nose with your own shortcomings, we could all feel quite confident that the experience of parenthood was a gold-edged, rock-solid guarantee that we would end up humble.

Of course, humility means a whole lot more.

Humility isn't a virtue that our society seems to think much of. Most often, *humble* has become a polite synonym for *poor*, and when it's used at all, it leaves overtones of homespun plain living and nostalgia for a simpler life. The nostalgia is probably for a past that is farther removed than we realize: Even back in the middle of the nineteenth century, Charles Dickens was poking fun at humility with his character Uriah Heep, who bobbed and bowed through *David Copperfield*, assuring all and sundry that he was the "'umblest" person going. (His mother was likewise a very 'umble person, he added.

They had a very 'umble home.) Probably influenced by Uriah Heep and his like, even my modern dictionary remarks that the word *humility,* while suggesting a virtue, may also imply undue self-depreciation, and offers *insignificant* as a synonym. Close by *humility* in the dictionary there is also *humiliation*—a word with which we are probably more familiar on an everyday basis—which sounds a little too close for comfort.

So why in the world should we attach much value to humility?

Well, for one thing, the Lord appears to think it's important. References to humility thread like a leitmotif through the Old Testament and the Book of Mormon, and Jesus' teachings on the subject were powerful enough that both Matthew and Luke recorded virtually the same words: "For whosoever exalteth himself shall be abased; and he that humbleth himself shall be exalted" (Luke 14:11; see also Matthew 23:12 and Luke 18:14). Whether or not the connection appears immediately clear to us, humility is a vital step on the path of progression.

So the Lord gave us children to make sure we get going on it.

Humility means a lot of things. It means not getting carried away with your own importance, which is as important in parenting as it is in any other human endeavor. It means being receptive to all the commandments, instead of coming up with seventy-three good reasons why any one particular commandment doesn't apply to you. It means being prepared to see merit in the virtues of others, even if those virtues happen not to be ones you possess. It means being ready to listen to other people, instead of just waiting for them to pause so you can tell them what you think. It means recognizing your need for the Lord's hand in your life even when everything is going splendidly, instead of only acknowledging your dependence when things have gotten into a mess and you need some help to get back on your feet. Having children is an excellent way to be forced into learning all of these things.

Most of all, I suppose, what I think the Lord is teaching me about humility through the exhilarations and exasperations of dealing with my children is the continuing necessity to be teachable, open-minded, and flexible. Sometimes I recognize the lessons first time around, but I'm afraid much more frequently I have to fall flat on my face to be reminded of where I am and what I should be up to. Maybe that's why I was blessed with the children I'm blessed with, the ones whose behavior can be counted on to goad me into imprudent responses that leave me flat on my face at fairly regular intervals. Am I making any progress? I most profoundly hope so, although on the wet Wednesdays I have my doubts.

The being teachable part of humility should be easy but is harder than you might think at first. For one thing, most of us cling tenaciously to our own point of view on a lot of things. Having gotten started in one direction, we stump along with determination, not always pausing to look around and see if there might be a better direction to try. We get so locked into what we're doing that we might as well be wearing blinders. Maybe in stressing humility the Lord is trying to point out to me that it's hard to teach me anything if I'm so concentrated on my own narrow viewpoint that I'm not paying any attention. After all, the essence of being teachable is accepting that the lesson offered might conceivably be for me.

Wisdom can sometimes be found where you least expect it, and goodness knows, we all could use some sometimes. Say your current affliction is young Robin, who persistently grabs things away from other children. She's too young to express herself with great fluency (or to understand you when you do), but she is determined enough about her intention to take whatever she wants *now* that you suspect she's become a pain in the play group and the nursery teacher on Sunday seems unduly eager to hand her back to you at the end of church. Being firmly convinced that gentle loving-kindness is the secret of child management, you are continuing valiantly with reasoned persuasion, and Robin beams at you happily and then, being rather large for her age, swoops down on whoever has something she fancies.

So what if the firm-looking older sister whose children are long grown and who now and then takes a turn as a substitute in the nursery suggests to you that what you should try is a little less reasoned persuasion and a little more of the consistent policy of calmly removing whatever she's snatched from her grip and giving it back to whoever had it first? Teachability would seem to require that you genuinely think about what she's suggesting—not smile insincerely and murmur, "Yes, yes," while you doggedly continue on what you are determined will eventually succeed, no matter what. The danger with that attitude is the old danger of pride ("I know what I know, and nobody is going to tell me differently"), and all forms of pride throw you back solely on your own resources.

In anything as complicated as child raising you are going to need a lot more than your own resources. Maybe you have lots of reasons why her suggestions wouldn't work, but maybe what would is some amalgamation of your way and hers. It certainly wouldn't hurt you to open your eyes to a different way of thinking. Humility doesn't require you to discard your own point of view wholesale; humility merely means being willing to consider the possibility that you might not have the monopoly on all insight of any kind.

Teachability means listening to the Relief Society and priesthood lessons and the other counsel from the authorities with your heart. Not all of them apply to you; not all of them should. There are a multitude of people in all sorts of stages who need counsel, and sometimes it may be the brother or sister four rows back or across the world who needs that particular piece of guidance. On the other hand, it might be that the person for whom the Lord inspired that lesson or talk to be given is indeed you, and once you lower your defensive denial, you can see exactly how it ought to apply in your life. Or it's possible, after you've considered exactly what was said, that you'll conclude that talk or lesson wasn't for your use right now; whatever they were discussing doesn't happen to be a current problem. Teachability simply requires us to entertain the possibility that it might be.

Prayer, of course, is the touchstone of knowing for sure whether or not what you're being taught applies to you. Prayer is guaranteed guidance: Christ himself promised, "For every one that asketh receiveth; and he that seeketh findeth; and to him that knocketh it shall be opened" (Luke 11:10), and that promise is given not just once but in several places. The difficulty is that there is prayer and then there is *prayer*. Speaking purely from personal experience, I find that prayer comes in one of several modes. There is "saying my prayers"; there is praying-but-my-mind-is-really-made-up-already; and there is the kind of prayer that they're talking about in the scriptures, which requires me to pay attention to what I'm doing in the first place, be absolutely honest about telling the Lord what is in my heart (as opposed to what ought to be) and what needs fixing in the second place, and then listening humbly—there's that word again—for the guidance I get, whether it's exactly what I had in mind or not.

Obviously, what I should be aiming at is the third variety, but I have to say that, given the fact that perfection is still more of a fond hope than an actuality, I do feel there's something to be said for the first variety. Realistically speaking, there is a place in most of our lives for routine religious observance, and while it is clearly better for you to be charged with spirituality every time you go to church, or read the scriptures, or pray, it is still better to do those things as a matter of habit, if nothing more, rather than not to do them at all. I suspect part of the reason that we need to keep the connection open is that if we don't, it is so perilously easy to fall away and by degrees stop even trying to achieve a receptive frame of mind. Maybe it's Satan, maybe it's just human laziness and a bent for procrastination, but if I were to wait around until spirituality dropped on me of its own accord like a heavenly cloak, I would be waiting a long, long time. I suspect in my case I sort of have to prime the pump—and so I'm teaching my children to say their prayers even if all they have to say is to ask for the fire and the meaning that makes prayer what Jesus was talking about.

It's the children I'm praying about a lot, of course, and often what I'm praying for is to be guided to know what of all the child-raising wisdom and folklore I encounter I should be using in my circumstances with my children. There is an incredible amount of loose advice floating around out there, and whereas teachability requires that I at least consider what's being offered, there are times when what's there is so muddleheaded that I simply have to remind myself that I probably know more about my children than whoever wrote that article or is pontificating on some talk show. And if I remain in doubt, prayer offers me consultation with the one authority who always does have the answers.

Open-mindedness is similar in some ways, but for me it adds the dimension of reminding me that not all the answers will necessarily be what I expect them to be. For all we may resist our children's blithe assumption that the childhood we experienced is so far back in the glimmering eons of the past that we don't have the vaguest idea of what goes on today, open-mindedness, one of the manifestations of humility, encourages me to spend less time saying crossly, "Oh, for heaven's sake, they had television when I was little *too*," and more time with my mouth shut giving some consideration to the ways in which the world my children live in is indeed different.

To a certain extent, it all illustrates the French proverb "Plus ça change, plus c'est la même chose," which roughly means that the more things change, the more they stay the same. I remember learning how to hide under my desk at school during civil-defense drills preparing us for atomic attack; my children are given fearsome blocks of information about the earth's dwindling resources and the threat of overpopulation vastly outstripping our planet's capabilities to sustain life. I do have to admit that I never seriously contemplated the idea that an atom bomb *would* fall in the general area of my school (for one thing, no one ever suggested a remotely tactical reason why it should), whereas my children encounter genuine shortages and evidence of ecological damage: during the summer of 1994 we had temporary water rationing when a broken water main and pollution of a secondary source happened simultaneously. I was able to grow up with the idea that the cornucopia of plenty was infinitely increasing and would easily supply enough for everyone, with extras left over. My children are growing up in a more sober time when it is becoming evident that there are hard choices that have to be made by society. Of course, I can always reassure myself blithely that the Second Coming will circumvent much of what the secular prophets of doom are predicting, but generations of good men all the way back to the time just after Christ have been expecting that, and it may be we'll have to cope with some of these problems without divine intervention. In any case, that's one way in which the world of my children and the world in which I grew up are different and will require different preparation. I have to learn open-mindedness to admit that and to accept the reality that I may have to find out some facts before I leap to conclusions.

Humility—and specifically open-mindedness—may require us as parents to come to terms with the idea that our children's ambitions for themselves may not match our ambitions for them. Sometimes it's a matter of abilities, and we just have to recognize that whether they've got a load of our genes or not, their path is going to lie in a different direction than what we had happily assumed. Sometimes it's more a basic question of free agency, which may be hard to swallow if you happen to be the kind of family where four generations have worked in the same business (or followed the same profession) and the fifth decides to design stage sets in New York or try the perilous route of professional athletics or some similar course which looks to you like pure insanity. We win in such a situation when we step back before we're forced to and find the humility to recognize that the choice is not ours to make (and also prepare to either bask in success, if that happens, or welcome the prodigal home without recriminations, if it doesn't).

Humility requires flexibility. In this, as in so many other ways, Satan is the perfect example of how not to do it. In the Council in Heaven, he was so convinced that he knew all the answers and so wedded to his plan (so temptingly shortsighted) to bring all of us back to the Lord unscathed by the experience of mortality and so determined to get all the glory for doing so, that when his plan—which was actually presented in defiance of God's plan—was rejected in favor of the Father's more dangerous but ultimately far more rewarding route of free agency, Satan flew into a temper and went to war. Flexibility is what you need when there has been a disagreement about a course of action, you have presented your case and lost the argument, and you then have to come to terms with what has been decided. As our children get older, we get lots of experience with this. Humility teaches us not to cling with grim determination to our original position, but to be flexible enough to look for the advantages of what was chosen, and accommodate ourselves to them. Flexibility recognizes that all the choices are not ours and helps us adjust to what is going to happen anyway.

Flexibility encourages us to look at our several children as separate individuals and not indistinguishable units in slightly different packaging. What worked for one may not be particularly successful with another. Carrie had a hard time learning to handle money, so you worked out a tight system of allowance and baby-sitting money allocation, with tithing and savings and proportion made available for spending all carefully supervised and overseen. Julie, who comes along next, was apparently born with fiscal good sense and, having observed the sessions with Carrie, has the system down pat without your even having to explain it to her. Do you need to spend the same amount of time and exert the same amount of supervision with Julie? Of course not. Trust me: you'll find plenty of other stuff to work on with her. Raising her and raising Carrie are not the same experience done twice; to show flexibility is not to be inconsistent but is simply to recognize essential, eternal differences.

We need to be flexible in order to adapt ourselves to the immaturity of the children we love and anguish over. We don't expect them to get nuclear physics down pat at the age of seven, but when you catch Tommy with the action figures that you know perfectly well belong to Stevie down the street, you may be a lot less forgiving of his inability to master the nuances of honesty at the same age. (There are, after all, undoubtedly nuclear physicists in this world who, although adult, haven't got it down either.) That same immaturity means they'll get a lot of things wrong over the years: they'll be mean to each other and experiment with the truth and cheat at Monopoly and be rude and impudent to their elders and betters (us), and if they're really stupid, even try a cigarette once or twice. Humility requires that before you fly into hysteria, you look back and remember the less savory episodes of your own growing up. Flexibility means that you behave like an adult with some sense of proportion instead of assuming terminal moral degeneracy. You correct and punish, as necessary, but you remember that what you're looking at is not a seasoned ex-convict but one of our Heavenly Father's younger children who, like all children, is going to experiment with different strategies to find out what works. Our job is to make it clear that the unsatisfactory strategies don't work; it's not to overwhelm the offender with a sense of moral failure.

It's not just the kids who make the mistakes, either. While they're learning to be children, we're learning to be parents, and it often seems as if our lessons are a lot harder than theirs are. We're expected to be wise when what we mainly are is confused. We're expected to get the answer right the first time, instead of circling around it so that the child gets mad and stomps off rather than waiting patiently for us to get our thoughts collected and say what we meant to say in the first place. We are expected to be monuments of justice, when what actually happens is that our discipline is erratic, becoming more severe when we're tired and cranky or when the offense is something we can clearly remember a little brother doing and he got away with it and that memory still rankles. We are expected to be as calm and patient with the children when we're in the course of a major squabble with a pig-headed spouse as we are when the domestic duck pond is smooth and serene.

Parenting *is* hard, and looking at it from the eternal perspective of the gospel makes it even more challenging. We're not just trying to get the kid to eighteen and out of the house (although that's a healthy assignment in and of itself); we're building a relationship that's going to go on forever. For the time being our relationship is one in which we have the responsibility for teaching and guiding and supervising. We are the door to eternity for them right now, providing the instruction and showing them the steps to develop the faith that will be the foundation for their testimonies the rest of their lives.

What makes the weight of responsibility tolerable is the trust that parenting is a job we're doing hand-in-hand with the Lord. These are his children, too, and we only have temporary custody. Sometimes the Lord seems very close; the scary times are when he seems far away. Maybe it's a question of distance that you've built in one way or another: you seemed to be so determined to do it without consulting him that he's letting you get on with it, to discover for yourself how it feels to flounder without the sense of his presence. Maybe it's the major or minor commandments that you decided were not all that important and could be bent as seemed expeditious. Maybe (and probably most likely) the sense of being on your own is simply part of your job of being here on this earth where your trust in him must be wholly a matter of faith so that you can be free to make choices that mean something.

However it happens, those lonely times when things seem to be falling apart are when we discover what humility is all about. We know we're making mistakes. I like the way psychologist Raymond Guarendi put it: "Humans make mistakes in even the simplest things they do. You'd better expect to err frequently in doing something as complicated and prolonged as raising kids." (*You're a Better Parent Than You Think!* [Englewood Cliffs, N.J.: Prentice-Hall, 1985], p. 30.) The trouble is that you feel so bad about the mistakes you make with your kids. Baking a cake from scratch that refuses to rise and lies reproachfully on the bottom of the pan is discouraging; realizing that you messed up on the allocation of hand-me-downs from the one source that your children actually look forward to receiving and that for once their cry of "It's not fair!" is absolutely justified makes you feel like a creep.

The important thing to remember is that whether you are really aware of it at that moment or not, the Lord is indeed standing right behind you, and if you turn around and make an effort (instead of just wondering vaguely where he might be) you'll find him, and he will be able to help you sort out the big issues and the little ones. It might not be a mighty voice from the sky to reveal to you whether the child is ready for toilet training now or in another couple of months, but there will be help. There will even be help in figuring out what to do about that enormous gap between theory and practice, between what you always thought you would do in these circumstances and what seems practical now, between all that advice you find on all sides and the reality of the little child standing in front of you. After all, nobody ever had that particular little child before. Nobody was ever you before, either. There are going to be answers that you can only learn from your own experience as you rely on the Lord.

And what *really* develops humility is the discovery we all make, which is that even when you become aware that you've made a mess of it, you can't retire from the field of combat to lick your wounds and feel sorry for yourself. The job of parenting goes right on, and you have to go right on with it. Say you've come to the reluctant conclusion that the permission you granted for your sixteen-year-old to go with an equally inexperienced driver on a nice wholesome picnic (but some twenty miles away) was unwise and needs to be rescinded. Okay. You only gave the permission in the first place, you have sadly decided, because you were caught off guard (which was probably not accidental) and saying yes seemed infinitely easier at that moment than going into all the reasons for saying no, most of which you only thought about afterwards anyway. However it happened, the critical issue is that it was a mistake and has to be rectified. At least you aren't coming to this realization when the excursion is already under way (although that is bound to happen to you a couple of times over the course of the average adolescence), but instead of being able to quietly repent for your error and do better in the future, you have to confront the child in question now (unless you can persuade your spouse to play bad cop) and deliver the revised decision. The child in question is not going to be pleased. There's going to be a lot of tedious discussion about promises and keeping your word and people believing what other people say and it all being your fault. What you want to do is retreat to your room and maybe put a pillow over your head until it all blows over, but that is not an available option. What you have to do is keep saying, in as level a voice as possible, "I made a mistake, and I'm sorry. The fact remains that it's not safe and you may not go."

It is highly unlikely you can escape from such a confrontation without having developed significant humility, at least in terms of having been forced to abandon the pretense that you are the all-knowing parent. It's unlikely that the child in question really believed that anymore anyway, but it still isn't pleasant having the point rubbed in so forcefully. The growth in humility comes from accepting that being embarrassed about the whole situation is not grounds for getting grumpy and losing your temper and stamping off. After all, the outrage is understandable, as long as it's expressed in civil terms. What you have to do now, while sticking to your revised position, is freely admit that it was your mistake in the first place and explain that you're sorry (as the stores say about misprints in ads) for any inconvenience that may have been caused. It's asking for unrealistic maturity to hope that the child in question is going to be understanding enough to tell you, "Yeah, I know these things happen."

Our kids expect us to get it right every time (which I guess is flattering, if you think about it) and are incensed when we make a misstep. We expect ourselves to get it right every time and are discouraged when we get it wrong, which we will. Hopefully what we gain out of the whole encounter is greater realism about who we are and where we are—children of our Heavenly Father engaged in a complicated, demanding job that we're not completely competent to do. If we were, presumably we wouldn't have to go through this earthly stage at all; we could simply waft on a wave of perfection right past it. Whatever we were in the premortal state, it's obvious that we had growing still to do, because that's what we came here to do—grow.

The strength of humility is that it saves us from the sin of relying entirely on our own resources. The benefit of parenthood is that it is guaranteed to teach us humility. We get dazzled by the faith and trust our children have in us, and the temptation is to believe, as they do at least initially, in our own omnipotence. Over and over, we get caught on the crest of overconfidence and slammed down to the discovery that what should have, would have, could have worked didn't, and we have to go back to first principles again. Sometimes the children won't notice that we got caught flat-footed, and a lot of the time they will. The point of humility is coming to see that whichever way it happens doesn't ultimately matter; what matters is that we are never too proud to face our own errors and to ask for the Lord's help in fixing whatever's fixable.

Humility's a funny thing. What humility really requires from us is realism. To be humble is not necessarily to see yourself as a person who has little value and botches things up. That's not being realistic. It is quite possible to be humble and be aware of the fact that there are things you do well—as long as you are also aware of the fact that your talents are blessings and responsibilities given to you and that it is part of your stewardship to develop them. To think you are not capable of succeeding at being a parent (or any other worthy goal) is not humility, it's despair. We are all capable of making bad choices, it's quite true, but we are equally capable of making good ones. Parenting gives us the opportunity, day in, day out, of having to make a ton of choices, and some of them will be winners and some won't. As we gain in humility we recognize our capacity for making both kinds, and neither unduly castigate nor congratulate ourselves. We just keep trying to make more of the good ones.

Humility is an elusive goal. It's not usually the sort of thing we set out to work on: we are more likely to encounter our need for it on our way to accomplishing something else. In his *Autobiography* Benjamin Franklin talks about his own determination to acquire moral perfection. He says he started out working on things like temperance and order and resolution and frugality, taking one virtue at a time and concentrating on it, keeping track every evening of how he was doing, but a friend suggested to him that he should possibly add humility to his list. The friend apparently cited examples of Franklin's prior behavior which convinced Franklin of his probable need for it, and so he did indeed add humility.

He says he got along quite well on most of them, although order gave him some problems. ("In Truth," he admits, "I found myself incorrigible with respect to *Order*.") Humility was another pothole. "I cannot boast of much Success in acquiring the *Reality* of this Virtue," Franklin writes; "but I had a good deal with regard to the *Appearance* of it." He says he did manage to learn not to express himself in dogmatical terms, and to offer others the courtesy of never contradicting them abruptly but merely suggesting that in certain circumstances or cases their opinions would be right but that in the present case there appeared to him to be some difference, and so

forth. (Not a bad way of coping with the arrogance of adolescence, it occurs to me in passing.) But, mourns
Franklin, "in reality there is perhaps no one of our natural Passions so hard to subdue as *Pride*. Disguise it,
struggle with it, beat it down, stifle it, mortify it as much
as one pleases, it is still alive, and will every now and
then peep out and show itself. You will see it perhaps
often in this History. For even if I could conceive that I
had completely overcome it, I should probably be proud
of my Humility." (In *The Norton Anthology of American
Literature*, ed. Nina Baym et al., 3d ed., 2 vols. [New York:
W. W. Norton & Company, 1989], 1:467, 469.)

Parental pride comes winging around when we least
expect it. It's parental pride when we gaze around compla-
cently at the (temporarily) good behavior of our own little
flock of children and then contemplate, with narrowed
eyes, the difficulties someone else is having with theirs.
There's a couple of problems with that: first of all, there's
the old business about judging not, on the sensible
grounds that you have more than enough to do keeping
your own patch in order; and second, there's the fallacy of
treating children like products. Sure, the likelihood that
your children will be sensible and responsible and behave
themselves increases with your own righteousness and
parental wisdom. But your behavior is not the governing
factor. Their free agency is. Church history, if nothing
else, should convince you that parents of great personal
worthiness have had children who chose to live their lives
differently. Was this a sorrow to their parents? Very likely.
Was there anything their parents could have done differently? Also likely—we all of us have second thoughts. Is it
therefore a reflection on them? Not unless we are going to
assume they possess power and authority that the Lord
hasn't given anyone else. You can teach and you can
guide, but in the end, you cannot make the decisions.
Your children do that.

Each child arrives in the world uniquely packaged,
with individuality established on arrival. There have been
longitudinal studies demonstrating that infants differ in

activity level, regularity, approach or withdrawal, adaptability to change in routine, positive or negative mood, and intensity of response, among numerous other aspects of behavior. It seems only reasonable that some of us arrive here more or less inclined to various attitudes towards spirituality as well. Some of us are lucky: we get the babies who produce the behavior which is generally most convenient for the adults around them, which is to say they lie placidly in one spot like a bedding plant, producing a predictable smile whenever somebody leans over to say hello, and they grow up to beam at their Sunday School teachers and bear their testimonies. It is only natural to assume that such obliging behavior is a direct result of our natural talent for parenting. Others get the active, squirmy kind whose insides don't seem to settle down comfortably to a post-uterine environment and who fret and wail to express dissatisfaction with the new order of things. Sometimes they go on being restless and squirmy and grow up to pull the hair of the kids sitting in front of them and ask questions aggressively (which may not be an entirely bad thing, as long as they listen to the answers). The mothers and fathers blessed with these cranky babies are more inclined to get started on feeling humble early in their parental career: it seems absolutely obvious that they're doing *something* wrong or the baby would be happy.

The one conclusion is no more logical than the other. It's true that a confident, easygoing caretaker can calm down a baby who might otherwise be a little restless, and that one who is tense and anxious can produce a fidgety child, but it's also easy to determine from just looking around that a mother who is so placid she is a short step from being comatose may have a live wire (which will probably wake her up, if nothing else), and that the edgy mothers are occasionally blessed with children who spend the rest of their lives murmuring, "Come on, Mom, don't get so uptight. It's under control." I remember reading once that whereas we as parents make an impression on our children, it's not necessarily the molding that we think we're doing. Instead of being like sculptors in control of a block of clay, it's more like falling down on a pile of it. The impression that's left when we get up is unquestionably our impression; it just may not be precisely what we had in mind.

Parental humility means coming to terms with that reality and recognizing that we are parenting in partnership with the Lord. I don't expect it always comes out the way he would have it come, either. How else do you account for the human oddities like the Marquis de Sade and Hitler and others of their ilk who found pleasure and satisfaction in the suffering of others? In the end, as parents and as fellow spirit children of our Heavenly Father, we have to recognize that our children have their own identity and integrity and so do we. Part of our job will be learning to adapt ourselves to each other: maybe you'll discover that you're more patient than you ever thought you would be, or maybe you'll find that you lose your temper more easily; maybe you'll find that you can bob contentedly on a sea of change, or maybe you'll find you're continually grasping for some constant somewhere and discover you're praying a lot for stability in what feels to you like continual uproar. The children will learn about your funny little ways, the same way you learned about your parents', and ideally the relationship that you'll be building for eternity will make space for most of those idiosyncrasies. (It's nice to think that even in eternity you'll still be able to be amused at your mother's way of fussing that everybody is comfortable enough or your father's insatiable curiosity.) We can love each other dearly, but we can't take charge of another spirit in this life or any other.

The whole point of humility, after all, is to enable us to move toward self-forgetfulness and, in that freedom, to deal openly and justly with everyone else around us, not just the children. Pride keeps our eyes turned inward, contemplating our own competence or skill or brilliance, not noticing what's really going on because we're so busy admiring ourselves. By giving us stubborn, argumentative, fidgety children to be responsible for, the Lord guarantees that we are jolted out of our peaceful self-satisfaction. I suppose it is possible to remain convinced of your own excellence when parenting a child, but I sure think it would take a lot of denial and episodes of amnesia. Children keep us humble because children keep reminding us that we are fallible, comical, too quick to speak, and too slow to figure out what was really happening. As long as we can keep the faith that all those things are probably true (but not catastrophic as long as we can keep a grip on love, our capacity for improvement, and our sense of humor) and keep our attention firmly fixed on the problems at hand and not necessarily our own reactions to them, we're going to be fine.

With humility, we are free. Knowing our hand is in the hand of the Lord, we can sit back, on the good days, and with his comforting presence, watch the children flower. We may not have done it all, but we were there. Humbly, realistically, that's not half bad.

7

Love

*The Way,
the Truth,
and the Life*

Love is something we all know something about. For
one thing, loving and being loved is one of the nicest aspects of life in this world, giving us a reason to keep on
with the harder parts. For another, living in the time and
place we do, love is pretty close to inescapable. We read
about love in our magazines and our books, and we see
love stories retold in a dozen different ways on the big
screen and the little screen at home. The songs we listen
to and the ones we flip past on the radio are full of it,
too—lyrical love, angry love, crude love. Love may not
make the world go round, but it sure keeps it company.

Of course, what most of that is about is romantic love.
Only occasionally are the songs or stories about the sometimes tender, sometimes fierce nurturing love of parents

for their children, which is probably one of the reasons that parental love takes us by surprise. It's not that we're not prepared for the idea that we'll love our children; we simply don't expect what it feels like to hold a baby in our arms and have that baby be *ours.* It doesn't matter if it's red-faced or slightly squashed or bald or has hair sticking in every conceivable direction: this one is different from every other baby ever born. This one belongs to you.

The intensity of that connection is what makes child raising so rewarding and so hard. Love of our children is, in a lot of ways, a tug-of-war. On the one side, we want to leap in and protect them from every evil. We want to keep them safe under a sheltering wing, to surround them with all the good things, and to ward away the dangers. On the other, we know it's our job to prepare them for life on their own, and no matter how passionately we feel that they belong to us, we know we can never possess them. They are separate from us. We want them to be free to be everything we believe they can be. Ultimately, they will have their own successes and their own failures, and the best we can do is help them be strong enough and sure enough to face either.

Love complicates all of that, just the way love complicates marriage. In both relationships, love has to be broad and deep enough to take in the good and the bad alike. With marriage, we're apt to start out programmed for perfection. We begin by falling deeply, romantically in love, and then we marry and we find that the person we married is sometimes grouchy or doesn't always listen before speaking or spends money more casually than seems reasonable or has a passion for order that's going to drive you crazy. Unfortunately, the contemporary temptation in our wider society appears to be to decide that if it's really getting under your skin, maybe the whole thing was a mistake and you should look for somebody different so you won't have those problems. Of course, that might be quite successful. The next time you would know what to look out for. On the other hand, the somebody different might turn out to veer nervously away from any disagreement so you never get anything settled or be so closemouthed you worry about what's going on or so careful with money that deciding to go to a movie becomes a major fiscal decision or so casual about mutual possessions that you are faced with the charming alternatives of spending hours hunting for things or spending a small fortune replacing them. Such are the advantages of change. The rewards of stability take longer to discover, but at least one of them is that you've already found out the downside of whatever you're dealing with.

Much the same sort of thing happens with our children, only we don't have the option of divorcing them. We start out with what look like wide-eyed, malleable babies and discover what they grow up into is a cross-section of human possibilities. Depending on the individual child, they are stubborn, easygoing, generous, self-centered, thoughtful, jealous, and all the other things we can be. With them, we have to learn what the wisdom of past generations has always taught about any lifelong relationship: the fabric is made up, warp and woof, of some things that delight and warm your heart and of some things that you would change if you could. The strength of love is that it can grow over the years to encompass both.

Which is not to say that we don't throw ourselves into a game effort to perfect our children, polishing and rubbing away at the rough edges, exhorting and encouraging them to emerge from the chrysalis of childhood into the glory of being well-rounded, capable adults. Not exactly just like us: what we're intending is that they get to be a whole lot better—practically perfect, in fact. The fact that we're still a step or two short of perfection ourselves, and our parents were, and their parents, doesn't slow us down a bit. If determination can do it, these kids are going to be the ones who get there.

All this adds a certain spice to the adventure of parenting. It certainly teaches us a lot about love. We're usually pretty young when we start out with our children, and we have a lot of learning to do about love's possibilities. Love feels easy. It's living life lovingly that's hard. The pretty pictures of love are perfectly true: you and your baby chortling at each other; you basking in the tenderness of cradling a sleeping child; the quick secret smile your child gives you when he spots you in the audience at the school program because he knew you'd be there. It's the rest of it you don't quite expect to happen to *you:* climbing up the shaky ladder to the bathroom window because your little dumpling has locked herself in; finally locating the child who went missing in the mall for twenty minutes while you aged twenty years and during your frantic search tried not to think about all the newspaper headlines you've read; getting so cross you are practically incoherent with your dear child who invited friends over to the house when you were not there even though you had explicitly forbidden it, and then in the middle of the absolutely justified scolding you are delivering she looks at you with such abject guilt and hope for forgiveness that your heart twists with love.

Love in its way is a dangerous business. It is the fundamental principle of the gospel, but opening yourself to love means making yourself vulnerable. It means giving up all your selfish self-protection and laying your defenses aside. Perhaps that's what Jesus meant when he told the Pharisee lawyer that the first and great commandment was "Thou shalt love the Lord thy God with all thy heart, and with all thy soul, and with all thy mind" (Matthew 22:37). He meant that we are to trust him so completely that we leave ourselves not a shred of distance for self-protection.

In other words, we are to love the Lord unreservedly, with nothing held back. We begin to see what Jesus was talking about when we think how cautious we are with committing ourselves to love in human relationships. It takes some people a long time to learn to trust anybody; in fact, one of the things we find so engaging about children is that they haven't yet thrown up the walls of protection, and they love simply and naturally. What Jesus is telling us, over and over, is that we have to find our way back to that childlike simplicity, and approach our Heavenly Father with adult faith enriched by openness and trust, like a child. Only then are we able to receive the blessings that, loving us, the Lord is so eager to give us. Only when we are willing to commit ourselves entirely, without reservation or stipulations, is there space and place to accept them.

And to help us learn that open commitment, he sends us our children.

There are certainly people who choose not to have children simply because they don't dare take the chance. I suppose what it comes down to is that they are unwilling to make themselves vulnerable. After all, it's perfectly true that children can expose you to real pain. Having children is giving hostages to fortune. It's not for just while you're bringing them up, fussing about them crossing the street without looking both ways, or getting them off the garage roof ("What are you *doing* up there?"), or wondering desperately if the pain in the belly is gas or deserved retribution for a huge tub of greasy popcorn and three candy bars and a large soft drink consumed in the course of one movie or maybe appendicitis and how are you supposed to tell which it is? For as long as both of you live, there will always be that lick of fear when the phone rings in the middle of the night and you grab the receiver, terrified that this time something has gone wrong. The hard part is knowing that there are no guarantees that it won't. Just imagine the heartache that goes on in any one of those Ronald McDonald houses that now so fortunately flourish near major hospitals. Those homes exist to house the families that have a seriously ill child and that need to be away from their own homes to be near the child undergoing treatment. Their existence is a blessing, but those houses are full of the pain that can come with love. Even knowing that your family is an eternal unit doesn't really make the anguish of watching a child suffer through a life-threatening illness any easier. If you don't love, you won't hurt that way, but neither will you know the growth and happiness you can find in loving somebody even when you know the loving is going to be costly, and the comfort in our Heavenly Father's love wrapped around you when you at last are able to genuinely and trustfully turn over the outcome to his hands.

Of course, few of us go through the long-term anguish of coping with grave illness or injury. Almost all of us do get a dash of the fear and worry with the minor run-of-the-mill stuff that keeps the emergency rooms of our local hospitals percolating. Unless you have astoundingly well-coordinated and cautious children, impervious to sudden, middle-of-the-night illness, it's practically an inevitable ordeal of contemporary parenthood. (At least we do have the emergency rooms to go to!) Your mind may be reassuring you that even if a bone is broken or it *is* appendicitis, it's not likely to be fatal, but there is nothing like the frightened panic that makes your heart hammer as you sit waiting on one of those chairs with your pale, whimpering child in your arms. No matter how efficiently the staff is working (or how fundamentally comforting it ought to be that whatever is wrong with your child is considered minor enough that more urgent cases are treated first), the wait seems to take forever, and against all logic the fear is thick in your throat. It's love that grows that fear.

Nor are those episodes the sum of all our troubles. You might be the wisest, most spiritual parents in the world and still have a child who chooses to disregard the values that mean the most to you. More likely, you'll be the ordinary, well-intentioned garden variety of parent, and your distress over the course your child is determining to take is doubled by your counting and recounting all the things you might have done differently in the years before that would maybe have brought you all to a different place. It is hard to face the fact that you may not have been perfect, but most of the time you did your best and in faith have to turn the prodigal over to the Lord. It would be so much easier if you could just cut yourself away from the pain by detaching yourself from the child, and there are certainly people who try to do that. For most of us, though, there is still the love that links us, and you go on praying and loving and getting exasperated and getting hurt and wondering and hoping and praying some more.

Maybe it's just as well that most of us waltz into parenthood lightheartedly, knowing enough about the good stuff that we can hardly wait to get started. We expect to feel proud of this darling little thing who's more satisfactory than any doll we ever laid hands on, and we do. Everybody else is excited, too, and makes a fuss about it, and there are piles of presents and sweet miniature clothes and too many toys (it takes us a while to figure out that a newborn isn't up to much in the way of playthings), and as long as the fact that you haven't slept for five consecutive hours ever since you can remember doesn't bother you too much, being Mommy or Daddy is fun.

There are all sorts of new delights to discover. I know I didn't expect children to be so wonderful to touch and to hold. People have been comparing a baby's skin to rose petals for hundreds of years, but it took having my own baby for me to figure out why: they both have that soft, smooth, silkiness that feels so delectable under your fingertips, even in the middle of the night. It's perfectly true that a baby can absolutely reek when it needs changing, but it's equally true that there is nothing quite as delicious as the fresh, clean baby smell. All baby smiles are a little accidental to start out with, but babies are quick learners and it doesn't take them long to figure out that one crooked smile produces paroxysms of pleasure from everybody around, and when your baby smiles, your heart melts. Their bodies are so solid and warm in your hands, up against your shoulder, cradled in your arms. Then they get older and you get to know the pleasure of the small hand creeping into your hand, the arms clasped around your neck. I have learned to relish the comfort of a chunky toddler's body against mine, legs locked around my waist. I have learned to love the knobbly feel of the leggy schoolchild leaning against me.

They start out around about waist level and steadily grow upwards—sometimes it seems they get stuck at just about midchest level, and then all of a sudden one day you realize they're clearing your shoulder, and if they keep eating vegetables and drinking their milk (even if they have to be summoned back to the table to finish it up), eventually they're looking you straight in the eye.

I didn't expect to love the physicalness of my children so much. I've always remembered what C. S. Lewis had to say about material things: "There is no good trying to be more spiritual than God. God never meant man to be a purely spiritual creature. . . . He likes matter. He invented it." (*Mere Christianity* [New York: Macmillan, 1952], p. 50.) Whether or not we believe God actually invented matter is beside the point. We do live in a material world and are meant to take joy in it. I'm not even sure if God "invented" the sensual pleasure of parenthood or if it just always existed, but I'm glad I had the opportunity to experience it. Even now, when my older children have grown past the routine physical closeness of parent and child and I have to settle for a flying hug in passing every now and then, I can look back at the old snapshots and remember the rose-petal silkiness and the comforting weight of them in my arms.

Seduced by our children's delicious charms, we find ourselves discovering the unconditional love that the Lord means us to learn. Unconditional love is so much easier to learn with our children than with anybody else because we love those children so much to start with. Unconditional love means opening our hearts wide, which is again what we're inclined to do anyway. Because they are so dear to us, we're more ready to accept whatever it is about them that we're working on changing. Every single one of them will have something. There are children who have a rough time with generosity, preferring to clutch their possessions to themselves. There are children who have to learn to keep working when something is difficult instead of impatiently giving up. There are children for whom being popular is the be-all and end-all, and they have to discover that you sometimes have to do things that are unpopular and comfort yourself with the knowledge that you did what was right. Or maybe you'll have the child who has a tendency to ride roughshod over her playmates, bossing them around relentlessly (which you discuss with her), and in other ways finds it hard to take anybody else's needs or desires into account (so you talk about selfishness, too) and then one day she comes flying in, face alight, to report she has just figured it out. Bossiness is just another way of being selfish, she tells you triumphantly, so she only has one thing to work on! At moments like that, unconditional love seems not only what you should feel but the only possible way to feel. With such earnest good intentions, what can you do except love her? We would certainly *rather* have our children be perfect (assuming that in their perfection they could tolerate our imperfection), but we love them anyway just the way they are.

It's encouraging to find that growing in your capacity for love can enrich your loving across the board. I don't know whether your love for the person you married grows and enriches your love for the children you have together or if it works the other way around; probably it works both ways at once. Ideally, we love the person we married just the way he or she is (at least most of the time, when they haven't just done something really aggravating), and the years together, some inevitably better than others, can give our hearts a wonderful elastic quality, able to take in a lot of good days and routine days and even the odd bad day and come out of it with the delicious familiar intimacy of a long love and tolerance that can help us get past the children's peccadilloes, too. In the same way, getting swirled around by the storms and challenges and (thank goodness for them) smooth patches of child raising can nourish the love of husband and wife. There is, after all, nothing more gratifying than seeing your spouse in the midst of the children, comforting or confiding or joking or just plain loving, and seeing the faces light up and the love that flows back from them. There is also practically nothing more comforting than shutting your bedroom door and, with your back against it, admitting to the one person who completely understands that you are going to go stark-staring mad if that kid does whatever it is one more time and you haven't the faintest idea how to prevent it from happening short of imprisoning the turkey in a box, which sounds like a fairly reasonable suggestion at the moment. Having had a companionable mutual moan, you can open the door and go back to dealing sensibly with the problem.

With our children, we experience love expressed and enriched in responsibility. Love in a marriage gives you some needed downtime. You can take turns taking care of each other and have times of abandoning responsibility in play. You can play with your children, too, of course, but the balance is never wholly even. I've heard and read a lot of discussion about the pros and cons of parents' being pals with their children, and the most persuasive argument, to me, has been that settling for friendship sells the relationship of parent and child short. You have responsibility for your children in a way that you will never have responsibility for your friends, and partially because of that responsibility, you care too much about your children for that relationship to include the casual come-and-go ease of friendship. You can let your friends choose their own bizarre courses of action and maybe shake your head and wonder. You don't do that with your children; it matters too much. You've known them too long and too well. Your patterns of exasperating and managing each other are too familiar to both sides of the equation. This is not an entirely bad thing. Do you want to be a friend, I remember one argument going, and be one of the friends your daughter calls when she has the baby, or do you want to be Mother and be the one she calls first?

I guess I'll settle for Mother.

I know being a parent gave me a taste of what it must be to be the Creator: this piece of life made out of our bodies takes on an independent identity, and it is our job to protect and shepherd it. I suspect few of us are prepared for the surge of tenderness we feel for this fresh, new person, so small and weak and so determined to get started on the job of living. I suspect even fewer of us guess then how rich and deep that tenderness will become and that it will go on surging within us from that time forward.

Part of the pride of being a creator lies in watching our children grow, watching their minds and personalities unfold into the uniqueness of being an individual child of God. They wore exactly the same stretch suits as infants, but Patrick, who came first, grows into the boy athlete, hungry for physical activity and deft in controlling his body and any form of ball. Luke, his little brother, turns into a juvenile mad scientist, avid for experimentation with all the amazing things in creation and untroubled by your not-wholly-unjustified fear that he is going to blow up the house or at the very least make it uninhabitable by brewing up noxious gases in the basement. You remain wildly partial to both.

You find that one child as she grows apparently needs a healthy expanse of personal space around her, and all you can do is love her from a distance, trying not to wring your hands and worry about what she's up to behind her wall of privacy. (Often it's the ones who were closest to you who seem to have to fight hardest to grow free, and as long as the echoes you're getting back from the rest of their activities are sound, letting them set the terms of your intimacy is probably the fastest way to regain it.) Another child never seems to have to fight that fight and goes on cheerfully confiding in you with freely shared details of what she's doing and thinking and wishing for. Did you do a better job somehow with that one than you did with the other? Well, not everything is determined solely by what you do, not even if by some chance you were the wisest and most virtuous parent around. Perhaps part of the growth in our ability to love is our growth in our ability to meet different needs differently.

It's true that we get a taste of being a creator, but, really, all we can create is the physical shell that their spirits come to inhabit (as endearing as that physical shell may be). I suppose what we really are are caretakers, holding them in loving custody until they grow up and past us and ready to take responsibility for themselves. It's probably just as well that we lack the capacity to protect them from all the hurts and harms that we would fend off. They have to get skinned knees and cut their foreheads just the way we did. "They bleed like pigs with cuts on their heads," an older, wiser mother from across the street told me the first time my oldest child tipped off her little wooden scooter and split her forehead; I looked at the blood flowing down her face, over my hands, onto the sidewalk, and clutched at the hope that maybe she wasn't bleeding to death after all. She didn't, but my good neighbor drove me to the hospital so that on the way I could sit with her in my arms in the car, which comforted both of us.

They hurt themselves in more permanent ways as well, and we have to learn the love that allows us to stand back and let them grow as they have to. We would protect them from all their troubles with an invisible umbrella if we could, and yet how much would we have missed from our own life's experience if somebody else had protected us? Maybe if you had gotten the job you wanted so badly you would never have been there to go to that fireside, the one you walked away from with the one person you would come to love and exasperate and share eternity with. Maybe if you had gotten into that course that seemed the perfect opportunity you would never have discovered your other talents which have brought satisfaction to your life and ease and comfort to others. Maybe if you hadn't had that accident, you would never have learned the patience that only convalescence could teach. Who knows what disappointments are going to flower into new directions for them?

When we are tempted to smooth all the roads for our children, perhaps what we have to remember again is the example of our Heavenly Father and Jesus Christ. It is in our love for our children that we discover the barest hint of how much Heavenly Father and Jesus loved us—so much that the Father was fully willing to let us try the wrong choices and make our mistakes, even though he had given us counsels and commandments to save us from our folly. He did more than simply let us take our lives in our own hands, of course. He then sent Jesus, who was prepared to go through the excruciating agony of the Atonement just to bring us the incomparable gift of a second chance, set free of those very same mistakes by his sacrifice which opened the possibilities of repentance.

Eternity goes on forever, but our life on this earth does not, and our time here with our children, as long as some individual days may seem, whips by even faster. It is always the happy days which seem to move most swiftly. (Why couldn't it be the days when you get up on the wrong side of the bed and everything goes downhill from there?) If there is any one power that we wish love would have, it would be to slow things down a little so we could savor them. Remember Emily in Thornton Wilder's classic play *Our Town*, who comes back from the dead to relive her twelfth birthday? She decides to start the day first thing in the morning, and there, before her, the day unfolds in an absolutely matter-of-fact way, her mother at the stove, breakfast on the table. For the first time aware of how everybody takes life and loving for granted, Emily bursts out, "Oh, Mama, just look at me one minute as though you really saw me. . . . It goes so fast. We don't have time to look at one another." (*Our Town* [New York: HarperPerennial, 1992], pp. 99, 100.)

Sometimes it's worth it to remember Emily and stop to take a long, deliberate look at everything and put it away in your memory: your daughter in her droopy pajamas (you really do have to take care of that elastic) spooning the last of the cereal out of the milk; the baby sitting on the bottom step of the stairs chuckling and feeding who knows what to the dog; your son, who is definitely going to be late for the bus again, wandering around vaguely looking for his other shoe. How many mornings have you all had together and how many of them will you remember? Promise yourself to remember this one.

If the gospel teaches us anything, it teaches us that at this stage in our eternal progression we see only a tiny, tiny sliver of the whole of reality as it exists. We can't fully know at this point what eternity means, but we do know that our time on this earth is a very special gift, one that we can keep for only a short period of time. We were sent here to learn what we can only learn here, and from the time it takes, you would almost believe a lot of it has to do with the practicalities of life: arranging food and shelter and keeping everybody dressed and provided for. I guess all those things are important (although Jesus did have something to say about lilies of the field and how they grow without fussing about such things; as he said in Matthew 6:25, "Is not the life more than meat, and the body than raiment?"), but one of the greatest temptations of our life here is to become so absorbed with those mundane details that we let the golden moments of our limited time together slip through our fingers. We have been promised eternity, but eternity is bound to be different. Even given the problems and flaws of our ordinary life on earth, this time was given to us for our good and our pleasure in what we'd find in it. It was given to us, in large part, to learn about love.

In fact, that is one of the most splendid aspects of the love we learn here, particularly the love of our children, because that time is so very short. In the beginning, it feels as if it will last forever. Surrounded by babies and toddlers, we get into what feels like an unchanging rhythm of meals and walks and pushing the shopping cart with the children grabbing at the groceries and baths and stories and tucking into bed. It takes your first child's growing up on you to recognize how swiftly those days swept by you into what is now the past. My own children are mostly still at home, and already in my head is the picture album of the snapshots we never got: Martha solemnly riding a packing crate in the backyard, since we wouldn't agree to stable a horse in the garage, presumably to graze among the petunias; Mali, short and solid and determined in small, almost square red shoes (she walked at ten months), trotting up the sidewalk after me; Marianna running across a sandy beach in a striped pink swimsuit with her arms stretched out, balancing, her hands spread open like little starfish; James trying to pick up a puppy to show me in the backyard, practically knocking the poor thing out with the weight of the cast he had on his arm at the time. I suppose what I am really remembering is the physical sensation of my heart flooding with love.

We love each of them most when we think about them most, and since we tend to think about them most when they're causing us the most trouble, we love our children for slightly odd reasons. Maybe you love yours most because of the quality of the artwork on the wallpaper, or the ingenuity involved in capturing seventeen mice from who knows where, or the stoic determination demonstrated by your daughter's deciding not to wait another year, as you thought you'd agreed, and piercing her own ears when you went out one evening (and no, you do not particularly want to know anything more about how she did it). Maybe it's the time she carefully washed the no-wax kitchen floor with cleansing powder that captured your attention, or the time he thoughtfully, if inadvertently, set your clock radio to go off at 3:45 A.M., set between stations at high volume so you were jerked out of sleep by high-pitched static.

For whatever reasons, we love them far beyond our expectations. When you think about it, they're even worth all the character we sometimes so reluctantly develop. Do we sometimes wish it could be easier? You'd better believe we do. Would we do it again anyway? Without a moment's hesitation.

They start out totally dependent on us and grow up and leave us behind. We never realize how dependent we become on them until we realize that as they grow up we have to change our vision of ourselves in relationship to them. To become a mother or a father takes a considerable reorganization of your image of yourself, and to claim that the reorganization happens automatically is unrealistic for most of us. Oh, we do gradually gain the self-control and the unselfishness and the patience and all the rest of the good stuff, but it takes a lot out of us. Of course we intended to turn into good people eventually; we just didn't expect to be catapulted into improving ourselves quite so precipitously. And then we have to learn to let go. The hard part is coming to realize how much we have defined ourselves in terms of them, and how as they grow into adulthood we need to regain our own separate identity so that both of us can be free.

Perhaps the most challenging part of parenting is coming to the end of our stewardship and stepping aside. We need to love them enough to let them grow around and past us, knowing that we will always be there for them, but also knowing that they need to take the reins fully into their own hands. It's kind of scary: as they teeter on the edge of the nest, ready to take off on the first independent flight, there is always the haunting reminder of all the lessons we never got around to teaching them. Even more haunting is the thought that maybe those are the lessons we haven't quite learned yet ourselves.

The years have woven us too tightly together for ordinary friendship, but there is still space for the special closeness of parent and adult child, and perhaps *friendship* would be as good a word as any other for that. When the fierce, possessive devotion of a parent mellows into the deep, lasting attachment to the child you have sheltered and nurtured, you have to call it something—but maybe the better word is *love.*

And what is it that we learn through this love? We discover we've learned the joy of unselfishness, the wider horizons of tolerance. We discover the rewards of patience and the firm comfort of self-control. Realizing with humility that we cannot determine their path, and that we can only serve as an example (sometimes, unfortunately, an example of how *not* to do it), we recognize in the end that the greatest gift, the only real gift that we can give them, is our love, wrapped warmly around them down the years and through the endless reaches of eternity. It becomes the truest expression of ourselves and our deepest loyalties: "By this shall all men know that ye are my disciples."

The love will change only in how it is expressed. Exactly the same devotion that impelled us to spend ten frustrating minutes on an already hectic morning hunting for the social studies textbook that is unaccountably missing (eventually discovered under the covers at the foot of the child's bed, but only *after* the child left on the bus, so you have to make a special trip to drop it off at school) will be redirected into driving a vanload of used furniture from home across three states to help furnish the first apartment. The support you once showed by writing out the homework assignments for the daughter with the broken arm you now show by putting up the friends she made on a summer trip (although she's off at college when they get in town), feeding them, and driving them back out to the airport. Instead of tickling your baby's tiny toes and putting the socks back on to keep them warm on a winter day, you're putting socks on your baby's baby.

Love lasts forever. We have been promised that. As long as we are worthy, the love we learn as parents will stretch out deliciously through time and forever, warming our memories of the past and lighting the path into the future. Love will still be there, as far as we can see.

And farther.

Coda

What Remains

Once upon a time there was a little girl. She grew up in a family with a father and a mother and two sisters and sometimes a dog as well, and sometimes she loved them all very much and sometimes she thought they were a real pain. As the years went by she outgrew a lot of jeans and tee shirts and Sunday dresses and eventually, after she got quite tall, she stopped growing entirely and it was time to go to college. So she went to college and afterwards got a job, and then one day she went on a trip and met a nice boy from England who had grown even taller than she had and had other qualities to recommend him as well, and so they got married and had four children, which is how I came to be a parent and discovered a lot of things I never thought about before.

I discovered, for one thing, that having children is being catapulted into maturity. Most of us start out harboring the delusion that we're already there; few of us expect the velocity of takeoff into parenting, the free fall, or the exhilaration. Being a parent is simultaneously infinitely rewarding and infinitely frustrating. We don't anticipate our own capacities for love and self-sacrifice; we don't anticipate the reality that we will be expected to maintain our self-control when we are so angry we have to walk around the block to work the edge of it off. We may have thought we were in control of our lives and on top of things before; having children means that we tap into the elemental artery of real life that pulses according to its own rhythm. We can't decide what kind of child we will have any more than we can predetermine the pace of labor and delivery; we have no way of predicting what circumstances life has in store for us or our children during the years we spend together. We may have grown up as active members of the Church, or perhaps not: either way, we will come to know what faith really means to us during our years with the children when we are so bewildered or so confused or so heartsick that it is only faith and prayer that sustain us.

When we have our children, we start to figure out how much we still need to learn. We begin, most of us, young and foolish and self-centered; we thought we knew everything about love because we had already fallen in love and gotten married. What we find out is that we didn't have the faintest idea of how much love can demand from us or how much love can give. We discover capacities for self-sacrifice that we didn't dream we possessed and learn to ride most of the storms with reasonable calm and what passes for aplomb. Some of the lessons come easily and some don't. Some things you may never really get on top of: all it takes is for your children to get a certain insolent tone in their voices, for example, and you go ballistic. After years of struggling, you may discover to your embarrassment that this trait ("Isn't that just like Mother?") has become a lovable eccentricity to your adult and near-adult children, and they quite deliberately do it just to watch you vibrate while they nudge each other and giggle.

Why do we have to go through all of it? Why couldn't we have just the good parts, the ones we like to think about when they're happening and remember afterwards? Probably because we would never get around to choosing to learn most of the things we have to learn, and unfortunately you don't learn much when everything is easy. It takes challenges to stretch us, and being a parent is a speedy, guaranteed stretching method. As long as you try at all, you are led along by love and the need to keep up with your unfolding responsibilities until you have so much character that you don't know what to do with it—or at least that's what it feels like, some days. What really happens is that you grow up along with your children, and no matter how much you become capable of, you are forever aware of the gap between what you are and what you would like to be—for your own sake, of course, but mostly for theirs. You want to do it right for them. They deserve to have it right.

And what are we supposed to do with all these skills that we spend so much time and exasperation and heartache developing? After all, the children grow up. They move away and they start knitting the threads of their own lives and they start raising their own children, and they only want a tiny bit of our wisdom, which is only fair because they need to grow by developing it themselves, just the way we have. But what do we do with it now?

Well, we've been told that eternity stretches out before us, and we have been given glimpses of what possibilities we may have, if we prove worthy of them. It would seem obvious that if there is any one characteristic of our Father in Heaven that threads through all that we know of his dealings with man on this earth, it is his tender, nurturing care for us. Maybe by sometimes struggling, sometimes triumphing with our own children here we are beginning to learn the skills that we will need someday as we steadily progress toward our eternal potential. Maybe then we will look back and see our lives here as the kindergarten stage, when cutting and pasting and remembering to share were jobs that took our full concentration. Then maybe when we see the whole plan in its breathtaking perspective we'll be able to laugh at all the problems that stopped us dead in our tracks when we encountered them here, and recognize that all that stood in the way of our conquering them on the spot was our own stubbornness and inability to grasp what the Lord was trying to teach us.

But all of that is for the shining future. There is plenty for us to treasure now, to count as our blessings in this time and this place. It's perfectly true that we give a lot to our children, but what we give fades into insignificance beside all that we receive. It's so easy to spend so much time brooding over the things that go wrong that we never stop to be grateful for all that goes right, like the child who is so afraid of being burned by the fire that he never lifts his eyes to look around and notice the warmth and the light that it brings. Yes, our children can annoy us, and yes, they can disappoint us, but most of what they bring into our lives is richly rewarding. For one thing, they love us in a wonderfully simple and undemanding way, and all of us can use all the love we can find. Then too they're new to the world, and they give us the opportunity to relive our introduction to all the excitement of life, to the thrill of things we've forgotten about or overlooked for years, like the funny way worms wiggle through the soil or the plop that raindrops make in a barrel or the drama of lightning across the sky and the rumble of thunder—or the sudden spectacle of a rainbow, with all its promise and reassurance.

Children want to know things you've never thought about. They want to know how long an icicle will last in the freezer and whether or not goldfish have eyelids, and so, because you're a good sport, you move the icicle out of the way for weeks every time you want to get to the frozen peas or reach for the ice cream. You set down the object that you're trying to glue back together and go with gunk on your hands to peer together into the fish tank to hunt for eyelids. The stories you remember vaguely from your childhood are new to your children, and while you may not be lucky enough to have them take to all your old favorites, when you hit the right one you may find yourselves both totally caught up in the experience as you read aloud, you remembering all over again the way it went and your child discovering it for the first time.

As they grow up our children want our help and our support as they experiment with new adventures. They need to have us there on the sidelines, and we need to know that it matters to them that we're there. Out of that mutual need will be born a lot of memories, of times when we were there when everything went just as they had hoped and of times when things didn't work out quite right and they needed somebody to commiserate with them and remind them that the world doesn't end when you make a mistake. Sometimes they need to talk things over, and sometimes they just need to know that we care what happens to them, and so we tell them over and over again, from now until forever, that we will always care, that they are precious to us in a way that they will never understand until they venture into parenting themselves.

Here and now, as we watch them grow up and take on the stewardship for themselves, it is love that will linger behind, enriching both us and them as we, parents and children, go forward to take on the separate responsibilities that lie before each of us. Throughout the eternities, it will be the love, and the lessons we have learned along with that love, that will be part of us forever.

We may have thought originally that having children would be a perfectly rational experience, part of the kind of life we've always expected to have, a predictable and manageable next step. What happened disrupted our lives, made shredded hay of our bland expectations, and enriched us beyond our most extravagant dreams. We were forced to come nose-to-nose with our own weaknesses, and conquer them if we could. We discovered all the ways in which we fall short, and learned that if it was important enough, most of the time we could reach just that bit farther when we had to. In fact, the whole experience was a lot like riding a roller coaster; once you're on it, there's no way off except straight ahead, and so you grit your teeth during the drops and fly high with the swoops and the sweeping curves. And at the end of the ride, there are two new adults to greet you: the independent child you've raised to make his or her own way with the help of the Lord, and the person you've become in the process.

When you've been a parent, you've learned something about the world and a great deal about yourself. To have had a child is to choose to commit yourself to life as a whole, the good stuff and the bad stuff and the memorable and the purely silly. You grow through the experience because you have to grow, whether you really intended to or not, and you come out immeasurably richer for it. To have had a child is to have done something important with your life, for now and for forever.

To have had a child is to touch eternity.